THE DIVE SITES OF
ARUBA, BONAIRE AND CURAÇAO

JACK JACKSON

Series Consultant: Nick Hanna

D1338736

CONTENTS

FEATURES

How to Use this Book

THE REGIONS

The dive sites of the islands covered in this book are divided into eight areas: Aruba, North Bonaire, Central Bonaire, South Bonaire, Klein Bonaire, West Curaçao, Central Curaçao, and East Curaçao/Klein Curaçao. Regional introductions describe the key characteristics and features of each island and provide background information on climate, the environment, points of interest, and advantages and disadvantages of diving in the locality.

THE MAPS

A map is included at the beginning of each sub-section to identify the location of the dive sites described and to provide other useful information for divers and snorkellers. Although certain reefs are indicated, the maps do not set out to provide detailed nautical information, such as exact reef contours. In general the maps show: the locations of the dive sites, indicated by white numbers in red boxes corresponding to those at the start of each dive site description; the locations of key access points to the sites, such as ports and beach resorts; and wrecks. (Note: the border round the maps is not a scale bar.) Each site description gives details of how to access the dive site.

MAP LEGEND

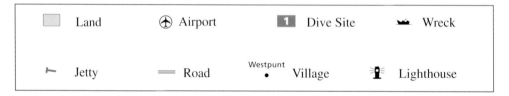

	Land	⊕ Airport	▮1 Dive Site	⚓ Wreck
⊢	Jetty	═ Road	Westpunt • Village	🛈 Lighthouse

THE DIVE SITE DESCRIPTIONS

Within the geographical sections are the descriptions of each region's premier dive sites. Each site description starts with a number enabling the site to be located on the corresponding map, a star-rating and a selection of key symbols, as shown opposite. (Note that the anchor used for live-aboards is merely symbolic: no boat should ever drop anchor over a reef.)

Crucial practical details on location, access, conditions, typical visibility and average and maximum depths precede the description of the site, its marine life, and special points of interest. In these entries, 'average visibility' assumes good conditions.

THE STAR-RATING SYSTEM

Each site has been awarded a star-rating, with a maximum of five red stars for diving and five blue stars for snorkelling. (Note that the author has graded the dive sites in this book on a world scale. When assessing a star-rating, readers should add one star to those given if they wish to compare the star-rating on a Caribbean scale.)

Diving		*Snorkelling*	
★★★★★	**first class**	★★★★★	**first class**
★★★★	**highly recommended**	★★★★	**highly recommended**
★★★	**good**	★★★	**good**
★★	**average**	★★	**average**
★	**poor**	★	**poor**

THE SYMBOLS

The symbols placed at the start of each site description provide a quick reference to crucial information pertinent to individual sites.

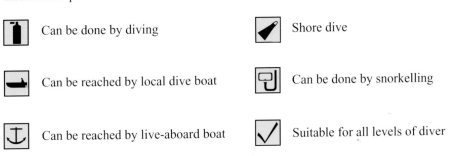

Can be done by diving

Shore dive

Can be reached by local dive boat

Can be done by snorkelling

Can be reached by live-aboard boat

Suitable for all levels of diver

THE REGIONAL DIRECTORIES

A regional directory, which will help you plan and make the most of your trip, is included at the end of each regional section. Here you will find practical information on how to get to an area, where to stay and eat, and available dive facilities. Local non-diving highlights are also described, with suggestions for excursions.

OTHER FEATURES

At the start of the book you will find practical details and tips about travelling to and in the area, as well as a general introduction to the islands. Also provided is a wealth of information about the general principles and conditions of diving in the area. Throughout the book there are features and small fact panels on topics of interest to divers and snorkellers. At the end of the book are sections on the marine environment (including coverage of marine life, conservation and codes of practice in the ABC islands) and underwater photography and video. Also to be found here is information on health, safety and first aid, and a guide to marine creatures to look out for when diving in Aruba, Bonaire and Curaçao.

INTRODUCTION TO ARUBA, BONAIRE AND CURAÇAO

Aruba, Bonaire and Curaçao – popularly known as the ABC islands – lie deep in the south of the Caribbean, some 25–80km (15–50 miles) off the coast of Venezuela and well below the hurricane belt. For several centuries colonies of the Netherlands, the three islands became an integral part of the Kingdom of the Netherlands in 1954. Today Bonaire and Curaçao officially comprise part of the Netherlands Antilles – which includes a second group of islands 880km (550 miles) to the northeast, namely Saba, Sint Eustatius, and the south part of Sint Maarten. Aruba seceded in 1986 from the Netherlands Antilles to became self-governing, though it remains within the Kingdom of the Netherlands.

The people of the ABC islands enjoy a higher standard of living than many others in the Caribbean; most goods have to be imported and prices are not always cheap. However, the Dutch influence lends a special atmosphere to these fascinating islands. The buildings, for example – rather than being painted light pastel shades as on other Caribbean islands – sport rich, striking colours: the result of a decree in 1817 by the Governor, Vice-Admiral Kikkert, who found that whitewashed walls hurt his eyes in the strong sun. Lying close to South America, there is also a tangible Latin influence, particularly evident in the local music.

Aruba, Bonaire and Curaçao are so near the mainland that on a clear day the mountains of Venezuela are visible. The islands are not, however, geologically connected to the continent, but were formed by ashes and lava pushed up from the sea floor. The climate is semi-arid and the countryside, or *cunucu* as it is known in the local dialect, Papiamento, is covered in thorny scrub. It is nearly always sunny, with temperatures averaging 28°C (82°F), though the trade winds help moderate the heat. These winds are very strong in the early months of the year and provide ideal conditions for windsurfing. The winds pass over without forming rain clouds, as all three islands are low-lying. Freshwater run-off is therefore minimal and the waters around the leeward coasts remain clear and calm all year round. The consistency of these conditions helps make the ABC islands a diving paradise.

Opposite: *Ironshore, or eroded limestone, is typical of Bonaire's coastline.*
Above: *The islands' flora, such as this prickly pear cactus in flower, reflects the largely dry conditions.*

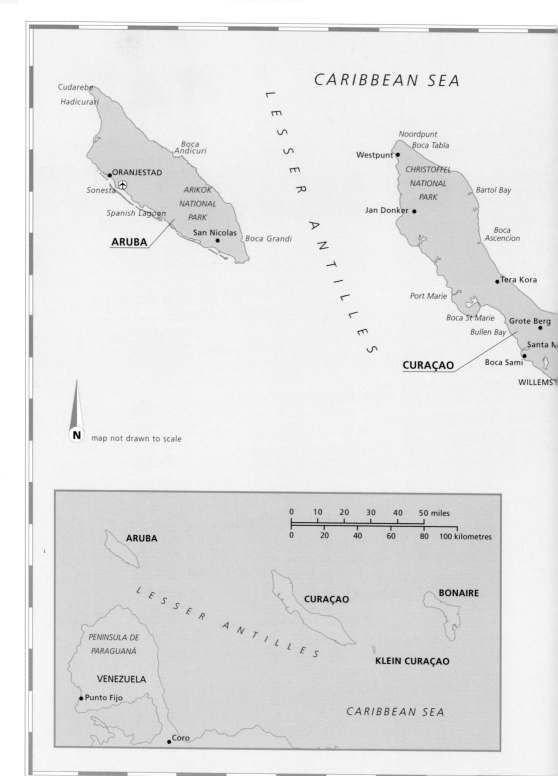

CARIBBEAN SEA

Cudarebe
Hadicurari

Boca Andicuri

Noordpunt
Boca Tabla

Westpunt

ORANJESTAD

CHRISTOFFEL
NATIONAL
PARK

Sonesta

Bartol Bay

ARIKOK
NATIONAL
PARK

Jan Donker

Spanish Lagoon

Boca Ascencion

ARUBA

San Nicolas

Boca Grandi

Tera Kora

Port Marie

Boca St Marie

Grote Berg

Bullen Bay

Santa M

CURAÇAO

Boca Sami

WILLEMS

L E S S E R   A N T I L L E S

N map not drawn to scale

ARUBA

0   10   20   30   40   50 miles

0   20   40   60   80   100 kilometres

CURAÇAO

BONAIRE

L E S S E R   A N T I L L E S

PENINSULA DE
PARAGUANÁ

KLEIN CURAÇAO

VENEZUELA

Punto Fijo

CARIBBEAN SEA

Coro

ARUBA, BONAIRE AND CURAÇAO

L E S S E R   A N T I L L E S

Noordpunt

WASHINGTON-SLAGBAAI NATIONAL PARK

Boca Slagbaai

Gotomeer ●Rincón

Boca Olivia

Boca Chiquito

BONAIRE

KLEIN BONAIRE

●**KRALENDIJK**

Punt Vierkant *Lac*

Lacre Punt

St Jorisbaai

Saliña

Jan Thiel

Spanish Water

●Nieuwpoort   *Punt Kanon*

KLEIN CURAÇAO

CARIBBEAN SEA

UNITED STATES OF AMERICA

BAHAMAS

CUBA

DOMINICAN REPUBLIC

US & UK VIRGIN ISLANDS

CAYMAN ISLANDS

HAITI

PUERTO RICO

GUADELOUPE

JAMAICA

MARTINIQUE

CARIBBEAN SEA

HONDURAS

GRENADA   BARBADOS

CURAÇAO

NICARAGUA

ARUBA   BONAIRE

TRINIDAD

COSTA RICA

VENEZUELA

COLOMBIA

PANAMA

TOPOGRAPHY

Curaçao is the largest and most populated of the Netherlands Antilles, and is situated between Aruba and Bonaire, some 55km (35 miles) off the northern coast of Venezuela. Aruba is the westernmost of the ABC islands, lying less than 35km (20 miles) north of the Paraguaná peninsula of Venezuela and 68km (42 miles) west of Curaçao. Bonaire, the second largest of the ABC islands, lies 48km (30 miles) east of Curaçao, 80km (50 miles) north of Venezuela and 129km (86 miles) east of Aruba.

Curaçao is approximately 61km (38 miles) long, 5–14km (3–9 miles) wide at its widest point and has a total surface area of 44,400 hectares (110,000 acres). Its highest point is at Mount Christoffel, at 375m (1230ft). Nearby Klein Curaçao is a tiny, desolate volcanic island 1^1/$_2$ hours by boat off the southeast coast of the main island. Bonaire, shaped like a boomerang, is 39km (24 miles) long by 5–11km (3–7 miles) wide, and covers an area of 29,000ha (71,680 acres). Its highest point, Brandaris Hill, is 240m (784ft) high. West of the main island, one kilometre (half a mile) offshore, is Klein Bonaire (Little Bonaire), a tiny circular island of 600ha (1480 acres). The smallest of the ABC islands, Aruba, is 35km (20 miles) long, 10km (6 miles) wide, and has a total surface area of 19,300ha (48,000 acres). Its highest hill is Yamanota.

Aruba, Bonaire and Curaçao all have a semi-arid climate, with the constant salt-laden trade winds producing a landscape of cacti, dramatic boulders and *watapana* (divi-divi) trees. Aruba used to suffer from severe water shortages. These, however, were overcome when refineries were constructed to process oil from Venezuela – with the refineries came the resources necessary to provide a secure supply of desalinated water, as well as a significant source of economic security for the island's residents. As a result, Aruba's population increased significantly, though so did its dependence on the outside world.

LEEWARD/WINDWARD

There is confusion regarding the terms 'Leeward' and 'Windward' when applied to the Netherlands Antilles. The locals refer to the ABC islands as the Leeward Islands and the three remaining Netherlands Antilles to the north as the Windward Islands – Aruba, Bonaire and Curaçao all lying roughly downwind of Saba, Sint Eustatius (Statia) and Sint Maarten in the trade winds. However, this is in contrast to another meaning that developed elsewhere in the Caribbean and gained political currency during the British Empire – where the terms denoted an island's position in relation to European ships' usual point of arrival in the Caribbean, around Dominica or Martinique. This second meaning is still used extensively in describing the Lesser Antilles and confusingly places Saba, Sint Eustatius (Statia) and Sint Maarten as 'Leeward Islands', lying as they do slightly downwind of Dominica and Martinique.

Bonaire's landscape features an ironshore, or eroded limestone coastline. This limestone often has sharp edges and can be difficult to walk across without hard-soled wet suit booties. Thousands of years ago the continental shelf, now located close to Montserrat, moved along this region and volcanic activity forced rock to the surface, creating the islands of the Lesser and Greater Antilles. Some of these volcanic eruptions produced molten lava, leading to the volcanic formations visible on Bonaire. Needless to say, there is no threat of volcanic activity on Bonaire today.

The most exciting feature of Bonaire, however, is its fringing reef. Many millennia ago sea levels were higher than today and the ocean covered the island, so coral grew on top of it. As the waters later dropped, the coral that became exposed to air died and formed surface limestone deposits. Nevertheless, the coral that was still underwater around Bonaire continued to grow, resulting in Bonaire's fringing reef. Off the calmer leeward side of the island, the reef begins right at the water's edge; with a tidal range of only around 60cm (2ft), live corals can be found immediately below the low tide line. Klein Bonaire, the small island off the sheltered west side of Bonaire, has the same geological history but with a land surface only just higher than high tide. It has not been developed, so its fringing reef is pristine.

Many beaches line the coastline of the ABC islands. Curaçao has no less than 38 distinct beaches. Some, like Westpunt Beach, are sheltered by towering cliffs and have become famous for high diving; others range from wide expanses of sand with modern facilities to small, secluded coves. On Aruba, beautiful white, palm-fringed beaches stretch along the leeward south and west shores, sloping gently toward the calm turquoise of the Caribbean. In contrast on the northeast coast, the waves collide with the cliffs, where they have carved out eight arched coral bridges, secluded coves and limestone grottoes. Bonaire is less known for its beaches – the best beaches can be found on the windward side, especially near Lac Bay.

History
Various Indian tribes lived on the islands before Christopher Columbus reached the New World. For the preceding 300 years it had been the Caiquetios, a group of Arawak Indians who lived there under the control of a *cacique* (chieftan) on the mainland. They mainly existed by subsistence farming and fishing, trading some of their catch for other goods. When Alonso de Ojeda (one of Columbus' lieutenants) and Amerigo Vespucci (the Florentine whose name was later given to the whole American continent) explored the South American coast in 1498/9, Vespucci referred to Curaçao as 'The Land of the Giants' because the Indians were comparatively tall.

Initially the islands were considered *islas inútiles* (useless) by the European newcomers. With poor soil for cultivation and no gold to be found, the islands were left to the Indieros,

---

> ### SALIÑAS
>
> *Saliñas* (salt pans) are a prominent feature of Washington-Slagbaai National Park in Bonaire. These areas of saltwater and mud are a reminder of the island's geological history. The sea was once 6m (19ft) higher than today, and much of present-day Bonaire would have been underwater. When the water level dropped, saltwater was left behind in valleys that silted up. Salt used to be extracted and exported from these salt pans, but nowadays the saliñas are good places to watch birds feeding, especially flamingos. The area of the *saliñas* varies according to rainfall, but even in the dry season the ground encircling them is treacherously soft and often wet; drivers should stick to the main roads.

Below: *Divi-divi trees are bent by the constant winds into striking shapes and forms.*

slave traders who dealt in South American Indians. Most of the local Indians were shipped off to work in the gold mines or cattle and horse farms of Hispaniola, while those who were left were expected to resist any other Europeans who invaded. However, in 1527 the Spaniards settled in Curaçao to breed cattle. The English pirate Jack Hawkins found Curaçao to be 'one great cattle ranch' when he landed on the island in 1565.

During the early 17th century the Dutch began using Curaçao as a base to harass the Spanish, and in 1634 the Dutch West India Company took over; in 1636 they built garrisons on Aruba and Bonaire to protect Curaçao's approaches. The Spaniards attacked Bonaire in 1642 but found that the Dutch had fled, so they burned the settlements. However, the Spaniards soon left and the Dutch were able to return.

In 1638 Peter Stuyvesant became the governor of Curaçao – and later Director General of all the Dutch possessions in the New World. Administering the Dutch possessions from Nieuw Amsterdam, which was to become New York, Stuyvesant ushered in a new prosperity based on the Dutch Fleets. The main trade underlying Curaçao's success was in slaves to work the Caribbean sugar plantations. In time, South American Indians were replaced with West Africans, and buyers came to Curaçao from all over the Caribbean. In the 18th century 40 per cent of all the slaves brought to the New World came via Curaçao.

Aruba and Bonaire were used as farmland to supply Curaçao, their poor soil being worked to grow maize. Aruba also became known for breeding horses, with Paardenbaai

Below: *Caiquetio rock paintings survive in various places, including Aruba's Arikok National Park.*

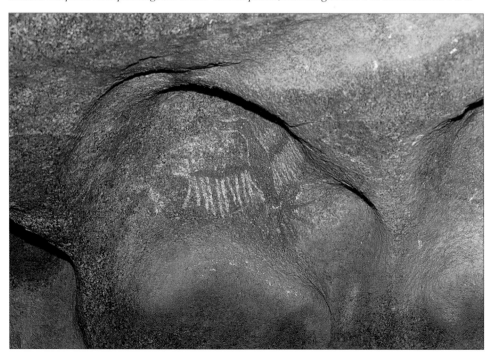

Above: *The tiny Alto Vista chapel on Aruba was constructed on the site of a chapel built in 1750.*

(Horses' Bay) forming the original harbour off Willemstad. Bonaire was home to some cattle ranching but its most important export was salt, an essential commodity before the days of refrigeration for trading ventures to far-off Europe.

Curaçao's fortunes varied with the politics of Europe. The British invaded twice during the Napoleonic Wars, but by 1816 the Dutch were back in control. Being near to South America meant that the islands were often used as a political sanctuary – particularly the closest island, Aruba, where Simón Bolívar took refuge in 1812.

During the 19th century trade declined and various schemes were tried to keep the islands going financially. Cochineal insects were bred to make a dye for inks, cosmetics and food colourings; aloe plants were grown for use in cosmetics and medicine; and sisal was grown for making rope. The salt workings continued in Bonaire and gold was found in Aruba in 1825; but Bonaire remained so poor that in 1863 the government offered it for sale. By the end of the 19th century the islanders were forced to find work abroad, either in the then Dutch colony of Surinam or helping to dig the Panama Canal.

The Panama Canal, locally referred to as 'The Ditch', reinforced Curaçao's status as a port, but it was the discovery of oil in nearby Venezuela in the 1920s that gave Aruba and Curaçao prosperity in the 20th century. With a stable political climate and steep shores that allowed the approach

THE DYEWOOD TREE

The original Indians made use of the dyewood tree (Brazil wood) long before Europeans found their way to the New World. Once its application for dyeing fabrics became known to the various colonists, it gained a commercial value that lasted until the end of the 19th century.

It was grown on all the ABC islands, though Aruba and Bonaire exported more than Curaçao. Because the tree was rarely replanted it is now close to extinction on Aruba. Nevertheless it is still abundant on Bonaire and Curaçao, especially where there is chalky soil.

In the 17th century the wood from the dyewood tree was exported to Holland, where inmates of Amsterdam's prison were used to rasp the wood for the manufacture of red dye (hence the name of Amsterdam's Rasphuis prison, or rasping house).

THE WEST INDIA COMPANY

The Dutch West India Company was a trading company set up by the Netherlands in 1621 to share world trade with the Dutch East India Company. In return for subsidies to the government, the company was granted the Dutch trading monopoly for Africa and the Americas, with the right to colonize. The company started colonies in the New Netherlands (later New York), Curaçao, Surinam and for a limited period, in parts of Brazil. The Netherlands armed forces were used to enforce the company's position and to plunder Portuguese and Spanish settlements.

The Dutch West India Company was not as successful as the Dutch East India Company. By 1674 it was in financial difficulty and was dissolved. A new company lasted until 1795, then collapsed during the French invasion of the Netherlands. Another West India Company was formed in 1828 but it too was unsuccessful.

of larger oil tankers than could approach the nearby South American coast, the two islands were ideal for oil refineries. Shell and EXXON set up refineries and workers flooded into the islands, increasing their populations by a multiple of five. However, the dependence on oil refining was short-lived. In the 1950s and 1960s automation cut the workforce drastically and during the 1980s OPEC raised oil prices, reducing consumption and causing a glut. The aging refineries, stuck with the ability to refine only one type of crude oil, floundered. The oil companies sold up and the islands turned to tourism to survive. Today, oil is again being refined but the islands have moved into tourism in a big way as a dependable income for the future.

THE PEOPLE

The people of the ABC islands are of mixed descent. Those on Aruba and Bonaire descend from about 40 different ethnic backgrounds and 80 nationalities, while the people of Curaçao claim descent from over 50 different ethnic backgrounds. Influences from around the world have combined successfully to form a fully integrated society on all the islands. Broadly speaking, the population today derives from a mixture of European settlers (Dutch, English, French, Portuguese and Spanish), Southeast Asians, South Americans and imported Africans. None of the original South American Indians survive, but there is more of their heritage on Aruba than on the other islands. On Bonaire, the harsh living conditions during slavery produced resilience in the character of the people and a richness in Bonairean culture. Less cosmopolitan than the Curaçaoans and less Americanized than the Arubans, Bonaireans are said to be the most Antillean of the ABC islands' people.

Although the official language is Dutch, the native language across the ABC islands is the Creole dialect, Papiamento (Papiamentu). Most speak English and Spanish as well. On Curaçao the population exceeds 170,000, on Aruba the figure is 91,000 and on Bonaire roughly 15,000.

CLIMATE

The weather is guaranteed to be sunny almost all the time in the ABC islands. The trade winds, mostly blowing from the east, keep the humidity low and moderate the average temperature to 28°C (82°F); the difference between daytime and night-time temperatures and between summer and winter temperatures is 2°C (3^1/$_2$°F). The hottest months are August–October and the coolest December–February, but the temperature rarely goes over 32°C (90°F) or below 26°C (80°F). The average water temperature is 27°C (80°F).

What little rain does fall, occurs in short showers mainly from October to December. Curaçao averages 550mm (22 inches) of rain a year, while Aruba has less than 430mm (17 inches). The average yearly rainfall on Bonaire, 65 per cent of which occurs between October and the end of January, is 560mm (22 inches). On Bonaire, the wind speed averages 12 knots, 15 per cent less than on Curaçao and 40 per cent less than on Aruba, with the wind at its strongest in February, March and June. Lighter winds and occasional reverses in wind direction occur during October and November. For most of the year,

Above: *A windsurfer attempts an aerial gybe on the flat water off Sorobon Beach, Bonaire.*
Below: *Aruba is lined with stretches of sandy beach, such as here at Sonesta Suites Hotel.*

ALOE

Aloe is a plant of the *Liliaceos* genus, which has more than 150 species, mostly native to South Africa. Usually they have short stems, fleshy, spiny leaves crowded into rosettes at the end of the stem and red or yellow flowers in dense clusters. Species vary in height from several centimetres to more than 9m (30ft). The leaves can retain water in warm and dry climates and their bitter tasting sap has a strong laxative effect.

When the green skin of the leaf is removed, a mucilaginous substance emerges containing fibres and the constituents that retain water. These ingredients have been known for at least 2000 years as good for healing wounds, sunburnt skin and stomach ailments.

During the 19th century the aloe vera plant was brought from Africa for cultivation in the Caribbean, Mexico and Venezuela. In the 20th century it was also grown in Texas, USA but frost killed most of the plants in 1984, 1985 and 1989. At the start of the 20th century aloe was widely used as a laxative. In the 1920s Aruba raised 70 per cent of the world's production, most of it going to England. Nowadays it is used as a moisturising ingredient in cosmetics, particularly hand creams and sunburn creams as well as being added to health drinks.

egrets and scarlet ibis settle down on Bubali Lake, the only freshwater wetland in the southern Caribbean, while Aruba is also a breeding ground for many sea birds and is the only area in the Western Hemisphere where black noddies breed. Some 45 per cent of the world's Cayenne terns nest in San Nicolas Bay in front of the refinery.

Bonaire is probably the most popular of the islands for birdwatchers. Over 170 species of birds can be observed, many of them at Goto Lake, Pekelmeer, Cai and Dos Pos. Bonaire is one of only a few places in the world where flamingo colonies breed, and the flamingo is the island's national symbol. They can be found at the Pekelmeer Sanctuary to the south, where the birds flock around the salt ponds, and at Lake Gotomeer in the Washington-Slagbaai National Park. The most common sea bird spotted offshore of Bonaire is the magnificent frigate bird. Its wingspan is the largest in relation to bodyweight of any bird; it is also known as the 'man of war' for its habit of tormenting other birds until they give up their catch. Other sea birds include the olivaceous cormorant, the brown pelican and the brown booby. Bonaire also has five different species of herons. The largest is the great blue heron. Other wading birds are also common, including the snowy egret, the reddish egret and the great white egret. Known for their loud cries, laughing gulls are seen on Bonaire in late March or early April. Least terns and common terns invade the island in the spring and summer, while royal terns reside all year round. Peeps, a local general name for all small shore birds, include the semi-palmated plover, the snowy plover and the semi-palmated sandpiper. On land, two birds are indigenous to Bonaire – the Caribbean parakeet and the yellow-shouldered parrot. Raptors include ospreys, crested caracaras and white-tailed hawks, while there are two species of hummingbirds: the ruby-topaz hummingbird and the common emerald hummingbird. Belted kingfishers, southern mockingbirds and bananaquits are also common.

On Curaçao 168 species of birds have been recorded, 51 of which breed on the island, 90 are migrants and 19 are seabirds. As well as the ubiquitous bananaquit there are doves, hawks, hummingbirds, troupials and yellow orioles; flamingos have their own sanctuary in Banda Abao. The parakeet and the barn owl are subspecies restricted to Curaçao and 14 other birds are endemic to the Leeward Netherlands Antilles and nearby Venezuelan islands as subspecies. The barn owl, the caracara, the white-tailed hawk, the scaly-naped pigeon and several species of tern are endangered.

OTHER FAUNA

A surprising amount of other animal life is also present on the ABC islands. On Aruba the boulders and crevices between the various rock formations create a microclimate that supports unique examples of indigenous flora and fauna. As a result, Arikok National Park is the habitat for several animal species that are only found in Aruba, including two snake species, the cascabel (Aruban Island rattlesnake), which does not use its rattle, and the harmless santanero (Aruban cat-eyed snake); the kododo blauw (Aruban whiptail lizard); and two bird species, the shoco (Aruban burrowing owl) and the prikichi (Aruban parakeet). As well as many species of lizards there are large iguanas, which are hunted for soup.

On Bonaire there are iguanas and lizards of all shapes and sizes. The large blue lizards are endemic to Bonaire, while the anolis, a tree lizard with a yellow dewlap (a loose fold of skin hanging below the throat), is related to the Windward Islands *anolis* species – rather than to the neighbouring Venezuelan species. The most common mammal is the goat, which may be found roaming the island eating everything except the cacti. All goats on Bonaire are actually owned by someone, and provide a staple food. There are also donkeys left over from hauling salt at the old salt workings.

Eleven native mammals are found on Curaçao: the Curaçao white-tailed deer, the mouse, the cotton-tail and eight species of bats. The deer, the cotton-tail and four species of the bats are endemic to the Leeward Dutch Antilles as a subspecies, while the baiomys mouse is endemic. The deer and all of the bats are endangered species – Curaçao is the only Caribbean island where the white-tailed deer has been present since pre-Columbian times, yet few of these goat-sized animals are left, despite protection from hunting since 1936. Nine species of native reptiles are found on Curaçao, two of which are snakes and seven lizards; four of the lizards are endemic to the Leeward Netherlands Antilles, while early Arawak Indians also brought iguanas to Curaçao from mainland South America as food. Herbivorous, they can live up to 30 years, grow up to 120cm (47 inches) long and change their skin colour to match their background. Females can lay 30 eggs in one year and the bright green hatchlings live in trees for the first year and a half.

Below: *Various reptiles, such as these iguanas, can be found in Curaçao's Christoffel National Park.*

TRAVELLING TO AND IN THE ABC ISLANDS

From Europe the major airline carrier is KLM, with services via Amsterdam from major and many regional airports. Other services include TAP Air Portugal via Lisbon and British Airways via Miami or Caracas with connections on Curaçao's national carrier, ALM.

From North America there are direct flights from various cities including Atlanta and New York, while other flights connect via Miami with American Airlines, United Airlines, Air Aruba, ALM, Air Jamaica or Guyana Airways. From Latin America there are regular services from Columbia, Guyana, Surinam, Venezuela and other Central American countries on carriers such as Aerorepublica, Avensa, Avianca, Aserca, SAM, Servivensa and VASP. Numerous connections are available from other Caribbean islands, including Saba and St Eustatius.

Aruba and Bonaire are also major ports of call on the itinerary of over 200 cruises from America and Europe. For more detailed information on travelling to the islands, see the directory at the end of each regional chapter.

ENTRY REQUIREMENTS

All visitors must have an onward or return ticket together with identity documents and sufficient funds for their stay on the island. Citizens of most countries do not need a visa for entering the islands. Those who do need a visa include citizens of Afghanistan, China, Cuba, Dominican Republic, Iraq, Iran, Cambodia, Korea, Libya, Mauritania, Mongolia, Burma, Syria, Vietnam, Peru, Haiti, Albania, Croatia, Serbia and Bosnia – except in cases where such travellers are in transit and staying for less than 24 hours.

All visitors are issued with an immigration card, which must be returned to immigration on departure. Length of stay is usually granted for two weeks and up to 90 days may be granted by airport immigration officials upon request at arrival. A visa is required for stays of more than 90 days.

A valid passport is required except by nationals of Belgium, Germany, Luxembourg, The Netherlands, San Marino, Brazil, Mexico, Trinidad & Tobago, and Venezuela, for

Opposite: *A boat approaches Santa Martha Bay on Curaçao's leeward coast.*
Above: *Car number plates on Bonaire draw attention to the importance of diving locally.*

DIVERS' BAGGAGE

Airlines vary in their provision for divers' baggage. Travellers from Europe wishing to take full diving equipment with them should note that KLM in London stick rigidly to the 20kg (44lb) baggage limit (unlike other airlines), even when a higher allowance is specifically requested in advance.

If time is not a problem, American Airlines fly via Miami or New York at a cheaper price and with enough baggage allowance to cover divers' equipment (including any camera equipment). The onward connections from Curaçao to Bonaire with ALM do sometimes charge for the extra baggage but it is a flat fee of US$10 not per kilogram.

whom a national identity card is sufficient. US and Canadian citizens only require proof of identity (although a passport is recommended) in one of various forms: a valid passport; an official birth certificate and a photo identity card (for persons born in the USA or Canada), or a certificate of naturalization and a photo identity card (for citizens born outside the USA or Canada). Non-US or Canadian citizens who are legal residents of either country must submit one of the following: a re-entry permit, a valid non-quota immigration visa, or an Alien Registration green card.

CUSTOMS

In addition to articles for personal use, persons 18 years old or over are allowed to bring in two litres of alcohol, 200 cigarettes, 50 cigars and 250 grams of tobacco. Ensure that prescription drugs are clearly marked.

HEALTH

A certificate of vaccination against yellow fever is needed by vistors coming from endemic zones. Vaccinations are not required for any other diseases, although typhoid and polio vaccinations are recommended.

Generally, however, tropical diseases are practically absent from the ABC islands (malaria is unknown), and biting insects are far less of a problem than they are on most other Caribbean islands. Remember that the sun burns, so come prepared with high-factor sun-block, especially if you are fair-skinned. The water on the islands is desalinated and purified, and is safe for drinking; imported water is also available.

Note that, unlike in Holland, marijuana and other such recreational drugs are illegal.

ACCOMMODATION

A wide range of accommodation is available to suit most tastes. Suggestions for where to stay in Aruba, Bonaire and Curaçao are given in the directory at the end of each regional chapter. There are also some condominiums available throughout the ABC islands. If you want to rent a condominium (or 'condo'), it is the same as renting an apartment or villa, sharing the use of facilities such as a swimming pool and any bars or restaurants.

The 'high season' runs from late December through to March. This has more to do with North Americans escaping winter in the northern hemisphere than the weather in the ABC islands. Rainfall is not much of a problem, and the ABC islands lie completely outside the hurricane belt, so there isn't actually any one time of year to avoid. The 'low season' extends from mid-April through to September. At this time of year there are generally less people and the prices are lower (sometimes dropping by as much as 50 per cent).

Regardless of season, hotels add 10–15 per cent as a surcharge for service and 11 per cent for room tax. It is customary to tip porters an average of 50 cents US$ per bag; other gratuities are left to the discretion of guests.

TIME

The ABC islands are on Atlantic Standard Time, one hour ahead of Eastern Standard Time and the same as Eastern Daylight Saving Time. To Europeans it is GMT minus 4hr, BST minus 5hr.

Above: *Oceans Bar and Restaurant is one of numerous quality dining establishments on Bonaire.*

TRANSPORT

Driving is on the right-hand side of the road. Cars, four-wheel drive vehicles, motorcycles (dirt-bikes), scooters and bicycles may be hired for getting around and a limousine service is available. Car hire companies, both international and local, are located at the airport, in the capital and in the main hotels. Note that only a few fuel stations are open late at night or on Sundays, on a rotating basis. International, US, Canadian, and European driving licenses are all valid for use on the islands. Generally, local drivers are extremely courteous, but be careful of the goats, donkeys and pedestrians that roam the islands' roads.

Renting motorized aquatic or land transport should be approached with caution. Some companies offer self-insured policies, so when accidents occur exorbitant charges may be levied against the hirer's credit card for repairs or replacement of the transport. Also, car theft, especially of rental vehicles left unattended (a 'V' on the numberplate gives away that it is a hired vehicle), is on the increase.

Taxis have TX on their license plate, but are not metered and should have a fixed price schedule for most destinations on the islands. Make sure you fix the price of the journey with the driver before you set off. Fares are for a maximum of four passengers and 20–25

Above: *A dive boat from Captain Don's Habitat on Bonaire approaches the shoreline.*
Below: *Many hotels have good facilities, such as the pool at the Tamarijn Beach Resort on Aruba.*

per cent is added for each additional passenger and during late hours – generally after 23:00, though on Curaçao fares are surcharged by 25 per cent between 20:00 and midnight and 50 per cent between midnight and 06:00. Also, US$1 is added on Sundays and official holidays and another one dollar if the boot cannot close normally due to the amount of luggage within. Tipping is usually 10 per cent of the fare.

Taxis can usually be found at any hotel, or ordered through the central despatch office when in Bonaire (tel 869 0752) or Curaçao (tel 8100). Taxi drivers can also provide a half-day tour of the island. On Curaçao shared taxis operate within Willemstad.

There are a number of bus services on the islands. On Aruba, buses run on a regular daytime schedule between San Nicholas, Oranjestad and the resorts along Eagle and Palm Beaches. On Bonaire minibuses run from central Kralendijk to Rincon but none go south past the airport. On Curaçao large blue or yellow buses run every half an hour on the most used routes. There are two bus terminals in Willemstad; the main one, serving the harbour area and the east of the island, is found outside of the Post Office on the Waaigat Inlet in Punda. The second terminal, which serves the hotel area, the airport and the west of the island, is by the underpass in Otrobanda. Private minibuses follow routes at the driver's whim – look for the word BUS on the license plate. Many of the main hotels provide their own minibus services to Willemstad.

SUNDRIES
Before your visit make sure you purchase and take with you antihistamines, anti-misting agents, decongestants, pain killers, mosquito repellent, suntan lotion, Swim-Ear type ear drying aids, any necessary prescription medicines, spare prescription spectacles if worn, and anything else that may be important to your welfare. These items may not always be available locally and will cost more as they will have been imported.

MONEY

The official currency of Aruba is the Aruban Florin, whereas the official currency of Bonaire and Curaçao is the Netherlands Antilles Florin (guilder). The Netherlands Antilles Florin is not accepted in Aruba, and the Aruban Florin is not accepted on Bonaire or Curaçao, although both currencies can of course be changed in banks. The Venezuelan Bolívar and the US dollar are accepted on all three islands.

Both ABC island currencies are pegged to the US dollar. The Aruban Florin is divided into 100 cents, with coins of 5, 10, 25 cents and 1 Florin, and banknotes of 5, 10, 25, 50 and 100 Florin denomination. The Netherlands Antilles Florin (abbreviated as NAG, NAFl, NFl, or just Fl) is also divided into cents, with coins of 1, 5, 10, 25, 50 cents and 1 guilder. Paper money is available in 5, 10, 25, 50 and 100 guilder notes. Higher value paper money does exist, but is not particularly common. Note that Bonaire follows a particular tradition in the way that numbers are displayed: thousands are separated from hundreds with a decimal point, and guilders are separated from cents with a comma; so, for example, thirty six thousand, one hundred and twenty one guilders and thirty cents would be written as NAFl 36.121,30.

Most larger hotels provide foreign exchange facilities, but with the economy so dependent on the US dollar there is little need to carry local currency. Travellers' cheques and US dollars are accepted virtually everywhere, even in buses and taxis. However, you may have difficulty changing large denominations such as US$100 or US$50 bills in shops and restaurants, and are likely to require identification and proof of purchase to change travellers' cheques. Buses will not take bills larger than US$5. Note that on Bonaire and Curaçao the import and export of local currency is limited to NAFl 200, and that the importation of Dutch or Surinam silver coins is forbidden throughout the ABC islands.

BONAIRE AND CURAÇAO ELECTRICITY

Bonaire and Curaçao have mains electricity supplies that operate on 120/127 volts with an alternating current of 50Hz. On these islands equipment designed for European 220 volts, 50Hz will require a transformer unless the appliance is of the multi-voltage type. Visitors with American equipment should note that this is not 110 volts, 60Hz as in the USA. American appliances with electrical motors will run slower than normal because of the 50Hz and run hot because of the higher voltage. Strobe (flash gun) chargers or other battery chargers designed for 60Hz may take up to four times as long to recharge. Power surges and brownouts are not uncommon. If you plug anything electronically delicate into a standard wall outlet, it is sensible to have a surge protector in between. Most hotels, diving operators and dive shops have transformers or controlled power outlets for charging purposes. There are only two cycle formats around the world, 50Hz or 60Hz, and chargers labelled 50/60Hz are usable anywhere without problems.

All major credit cards are accepted at most commercial establishments, even in supermarkets. Usually when buying with a credit card, your card will be charged in the currency of the issuing country. Occasionally, shopkeepers may charge the card in the local currency: if they do, make sure that the use of the local currency is clearly marked on the charge slip, and a special charge slip which allows the shop to select a currency next to the total is used. Travellers carrying Automatic Teller Machine (ATM) cards bearing the MasterCard, CIRRUS, NYCE or other ATM network logos can withdraw cash in Aruban Florins (on Aruba) and Netherlands Antillean Florins (on Bonaire and Curaçao). The home bank account will be debited in the currency where the cards were issued, though service charges will be deducted.

BANKS

On Aruba banks are open on weekdays from 08:00 to 12:00 and 13:30 to 16:00, although some branches stay open until 18:00 on Friday. Money transfer services are available via Western Union Money Transfer Service; for information call De Palm Tours on (297) 824400. On Bonaire and Curaçao banks are open on weekdays from 08:00 or 08:30 to 15:30 or 16:00. The airport bank in Curaçao is open from 08:00 until 20:00 Monday to Saturday and 09:00 until 16:00 on Sunday. All other banks on the ABC islands are closed at the weekend.

Above: *Pottery is laid out for sale in Willemstad, the administrative centre of the Netherlands Antilles.*
Opposite: *The imposing Queen Juliana Bridge rises high above the entrance to Willemstad's harbour.*

ELECTRICITY

On Aruba electricity supplies operate on 110 volts with an alternating current of 60Hz, whereas on Bonaire and Curaçao the electricity supplies operate on 120/127 volts with an alternating current of 50Hz. European 220-volt appliances and many South American electrical appliances require a voltage adapter (unless they are of the multi-voltage type) and a surge protector should be used for delicate equipment. While the majority of US appliances will run safely without transformers or adapters, electric razors and hair-dryers should not be left on for too long as they may overheat. Dive shops have regulated outlets for safe charging.

COMMUNICATIONS

The ABC islands all have modern international communications for telephone calls, including direct dial, person to person and collect calls, as well as telex and telegrams, email and marine telephone calls.

The international dialling code for Aruba is 297, followed by the local six digit number. When telephoning from within

NUMBERS IN PAPIAMENTO	
0	Zero, Nul or Nada
1	Unu
2	Dos
3	Tres
4	Kwater
5	Sinku
6	Seis
7	Shete
8	Ocho
9	Nuebe
10	Dies

the island you need to dial only the local six-digit number. Local numbers used to be five digits but were changed in 1997 to include the prefix 8. The international dialling code for Bonaire and Curaçao is 599, followed by 7 for Bonaire and 9 for Curaçao, then the local number (on Bonaire the local number is only four digits). As in Aruba, local telephone numbers can be reached by dialling just the local number.

Calls from hotels or resorts are expensive so it is advisable to use the other telephone services available. On Aruba it is cheaper to use Servicio di Telecomunicacion di Aruba (SETAR), to be found next to the Aruba post office at the Irausquinplein, at the SETAR Teleshop at Palm Beach across from the Hyatt Regency Aruba Beach Resort & Casino, and at the SETAR Teleshop, Schelpstraat, around the corner from Le Petite Café in Oranjestad. On Bonaire you can call from the Telbo building in Kralendijk, and on Curaçao it is cheaper to use the offices of the telecommunications company (Setel).

Internet access is available on Aruba through the Cyber Cafe, located at the Royal Plaza Mall in Oranjestad. On Bonaire there is an internet kiosk available at the Harbourside Mall in Kralendijk. The cost for using the kiosk is NAFl 1 for 3 minutes, and you need to feed coins into a machine to pay for access; plastic cards or paper money are not accepted.

Personal cellular phones will not work on the ABC islands (unless the personal phones are on satellite), since local cellular service providers have no reciprocal agreements with other carriers.

LANGUAGE

Dutch is the official language of the ABC islands but most locals also speak English and Spanish as well as Papiamento.

Papiamento (also spelt Papiamentu) is a kind of Creole language indigenous to the Netherlands Antilles. The word is a derivation of the old Spanish verb *papear*, which meant 'to converse', though nowadays the word is thought of as meaning 'babble'. There are numerous theories on the origins of Papiamento but it is most likely that it began as a Portuguese-based Creole derived during the slave trade from early contact between the Portuguese and West Africans in the 15th century. Since the Portuguese colonized a wide area of the West African coast, the slaves came from far apart and did not speak a common language. A pidgin language developed from African and Portuguese vocabulary, which became the mother tongue of a generation that settled on the ABC islands. The resulting Creole often served as a secret language shared by the slaves while not understood by slave owners who only spoke Portuguese.

PAPIAMENTO PHRASES			
Good morning	Bon dia	At the port	Na waf
Good afternoon	Bon tardi	The road	Caminda
Good night	Bon nochi	Police	Polis
Welcome	Bon Bini	I am hungry	Mi tin hamber
Please	Por fabor	Food	Cuminda
Thank you	Danki	Fish	Pisca
How are you?	Con ta bai	Chicken	Galinja
Goodbye	Ajo	Lobster	Kreeft
Me	Ami	Crab	Kangrew
You	Abo	Conch	Calco
I, I am	Mi	Salad	Salada
Miss	Yufrow	Bread	Pan ·
Mrs	Señora	Cheese	Keshi
Mr	Mener	Milk	Lechi
How much does	Kwanto esaki	Sugar	Suku
this cost	ta costa	Salt	Salo
Bank	Banco	Pepper	Pika
Money	Plaka	Soft drink	Soda
Water	Awa	Beer	Cerbes
Beach, ocean	Lama	Wine	Binja (*also* Purple)

Opposite: *Aruba's cruise ship terminal is visible from the footbridge of the Sonesta Suites Hotel.*

DIVING AND SNORKELLING IN THE ABC ISLANDS

Compared with the vast oceans the Caribbean Sea, a mere arm of the Atlantic, is minute – roughly 2415km (1500 miles) east to west and between 640 and 1540km (400 and 900 miles) north to south. Still, it contains more than a thousand different islands. Served by the Equatorial Current and the Gulf Stream it offers warm waters and a mild tropical climate, and is firmly established as the world's most frequented holiday diving destination.

The Caribbean was formed quite late in geological time. Some 200 million years ago, the earth's surface consisted of a supercontinent, Pangaea, surrounded by a great primordial ocean, Panthalassa, that covered the rest of the globe. Another 400 million years earlier there had been a proto-Atlantic Ocean, but tectonic plate movements had closed it. Pangaea, which consisted of Laurasia (Europe, North America and Asia) and Gondwanaland (the southern continents), slowly broke up to form the continents that we recognize today. Then three million years ago South America welded itself to North America, closing the Isthmus of Panama and delimiting the Atlantic Ocean. Cut off from the Pacific, the currents and species interaction in the Caribbean and North Atlantic were substantially reduced. Consequently the Caribbean has only a tenth of the marine species found in the much larger (and older) Indo-Pacific. Absent from the Caribbean are the ever-popular clownfish, lionfish and brightly coloured soft corals, but these are partly made up for by a profusion of other fish, gorgonians, rich coral reefs and colour from a myriad of sponges.

What the Caribbean lacks in species it compensates for in being diver-friendly. The islands and connecting ridges of the eastern Caribbean prevent the interchange of deep water from the Atlantic, so tides are smaller and the visibility good, sometimes approaching the near mythical 60m (200 ft). Apart from Cozumel's high-voltage drift diving, most Caribbean destinations including the ABC islands are relatively free of strong currents, and therefore well suited to novices and casual divers. Resorts throughout the Caribbean tend to be well organized and are often at the forefront of eco-tourism. In general, they have good facilities, introductory courses, a good selection of diving and camera equipment for hire

Opposite: *A dive boat floats above a typical ABC islands reef scene with various sponges.*
Above: *A mixed shoal of grunts and snappers shelter in the safety of a wreck.*

and a great variety of non-diving and after-dive activities, ideal for accompanying non-divers. You don't even have to get wet, as some have tourist submarines to take you down. Several destinations where diving is important to the economy have marine reserves, with fixed mooring buoys to minimize anchor damage.

For photographers, the Caribbean offers tame animals, maximum water clarity and minimum back scatter. And if the profusion of marine life is not enough, there are plenty of wrecks. During the Spanish colonial period the world's richest maritime trade was often prey to pirates, naval engagements and storms. Various 'treasure ships' have been located, while more modern wrecks are also regularly dived. Some islands have initiated artificial reef programs by sinking cleaned-up ships and aeroplanes.

> **DAN**
>
> The Divers Alert Network (DAN), based in North America, provides a 24-hour emergency hotline on diving related problems or injuries and recompression chamber assistance.
>
> DAN is a publicly supported, non-profit membership organization for sport divers and research into diving medicine. Dubbed 'The Divers Safety Net', membership benefits include DAN's Diving Accident Manual, their newsletter 'Alert Diver', access to special diving medical insurance and personal assistance.
>
> **Divers Alert Network**, PO Box 3823, Duke University Medical Center, Durham, NC 27710, tel (919) 684 2948

DIVING IN ARUBA, BONAIRE AND CURAÇAO

The waters around the ABC islands are influenced by the Southern Equatorial Current, which comes up from Antarctica. This current is full of nutrients that help enrich the coral reefs around the islands. The Equatorial Current later turns north when it reaches Panama and becomes the Gulf Stream.

Thanks to their colourful marine life and the consistency of diving conditions, the ABC islands are one of the Caribbean's top diving destinations. With majestic reefs, shoals of colourful fish, large pelagics, abundant invertebrates, wrecks, caverns and breathtaking visibility, the ABC islands guarantee an excellent diving holiday whether you are a snorkeller, novice diver, or seasoned veteran. An arid environment, minimal rainfall and a location outside the hurricane belt ensure that the underwater visibility is excellent. Among the friendly creatures you are likely to encounter are tarpon *(Megalops atlanticus)*, black grouper *(Mycteroperca bonaci)*, tiger grouper *(Mycteroperca tigris)*, great barracuda *(Sphyraena barracuda)*, and green moray eels *(Gymnothorax funebris)*. French angelfish *(Pomacanthus paru)* and queen angelfish *(Holacanthus ciliaris)* are common, while frogfish *(Antennarius multiocellatus)*, seahorses and numerous other small creatures are found.

Dawn and dusk are the times when predators are most active and several creatures of the night begin to appear at dusk. The ambient light in the water is highest between 10:00 and 14:00, so photographers using wide angle lenses may choose to dive hard between 09:30 and 15:00 and miss out on the afternoon's siesta.

> **DAN EMERGENCY LINES**
>
> **DAN America**
> Peter B. Bennett Center, 6 West Colony Place, Durham, NC 27705, USA; tel 1 919 6842948, 800 446 2671; fax 1 919 4906630
> USA and Canada and regional responsibility for Central and South America, the Caribbean, Polynesia, Micronesia and Melanesia (except Fiji).
>
> **DAN Europe Central Office**
> PO Box DAN 64026 Roseto (Te), Italy; tel 39 085 8930333; fax 39 085 8930050
> Geographical Europe, European territories and protectorates, with regional responsibility for the Mediterranean Sea and Shore, the Red Sea, the Arabian Gulf, Ethiopia, Kenya and the Maldives.

THE STAR GRADING SYSTEM FOR DIVE QUALITY

While the quality of diving in the ABC islands is high, no dive site in the Caribbean can fully compare with the best of the Indian Ocean, South Pacific or Red Sea for species diversity. However, dives in the Caribbean can make up for this with their ease of diving, the quality of the reef, fish habituation to divers' presence and any unique small or

ARUBA

American divers voted Aruba as having the best topside attractions in the Caribbean. Of the three ABC islands, Aruba has the finest beaches; all but one of which are public and free. Also the Arubans graciously welcome tourists and even though half a million tourists 'invade' the island for their holidays each year there is no hint of resentment on the part of the locals. It is no surprise that Aruba attracts such a high ratio of repeat visitors.

Expanses of beaches and solitary coves line both sides of the island, although there are fewer on the northeast side where the sea is rough and not good for swimming. There is a plethora of non-diving watersports, especially windsurfing and yachting in the 15–20 knot trade winds. The winds are so consistent that Arubans can sail to the coast of Venezuela, about 25km (15 miles) away, in less time than it takes by ferry.

Other activities include fishing, mountain biking, horse riding, tennis and golfing. Also, for those not inclined to get wet, Aruba's marine life can be viewed from submarines, semi-submarines and glass-bottomed boats. Rock climbing is available in the east of the island.

HISTORY

The first people known to have inhabited Aruba were Arawak Indians called Caiquetios who migrated north from the Orinoco Basin in South America. Remnants of their culture can be found at a number of sites around the island including hieroglyphics still visible on granite boulders and in some caves.

It is thought that the Spanish explorer Alonso de Ojeda claimed the island for Queen Isabella in 1499, hoping to find gold there. However, the name Aruba seems to have originally derived from Arawak Indian words, either *oibubai* (which means guide), *oruba* (meaning well-placed, convenient to the mainland) or *ora* (shell) and *oubao* (island).

The Spanish found the climate too arid for cultivation and failed to find any gold, so in 1515 they exported almost the entire Indian population to Santo Domingo on Hispaniola. Here they were put to work in the cattle farms, horse farms and mines, though twelve years later some of the Indians were sent back to Aruba to help protect the Spanish Main. During

Opposite: *The sandy beaches lining the leeward side of Aruba include beautiful Druif Beach.*
Above: *A lasting Dutch colonial influence is evident in the design of a modern Aruban house.*

the following 150 years the island became a hiding place for pirates and buccaneers preying on ships transporting New World treasures back to Europe. Fortunately, because the Spanish considered Aruba useless, the island was spared the usual horrors of Spanish occupation and the Indian population was not exterminated.

In 1636, near to the culmination of 80 years war between them, the Dutch, who had been expelled by the Spanish from their base in St Maarten and were looking for another place to establish a colonial presence, captured Aruba, Bonaire and Curaçao from the Spanish. Curaçao became the administrative capital for the Dutch West India Company in the Netherlands Antilles, with Aruba operating as one of its main satellites. The fortress Fort Zoutman, the oldest building on the island, was built soon after. There was a short period from 1805 to 1815 when the island was captured by the British, but Aruba has remained under Dutch control ever since.

Alluvial gold was discovered at Rooi Huit in 1824, with the ruins of a 19th-century smelting plant still surviving in Balashi, northwest of Spanish Lagoon. The gold mines yielded over 1,360,000kg (3,000,000lb) before they ceased to be economic in 1916. However, black gold (oil) was then found in the Maracaibo fields in Venezuela in the 1920s and the Dutch islands presented ideal locations for refineries.

The Royal Dutch Shell refinery was built along the Eagle Beach area in 1926, and in 1929 the Pan American Petroleum Corporation built a refinery at San Nicolas. In 1934 EXXON bought this refinery (the world's largest until 1968), turning San Nicolas into a major commercial centre: Aruba was the largest refiner of petrol for the allied forces during World

ARIKOK NATIONAL PARK

Covering 17 per cent of Aruba's landmass, Arikok National Park was first designated as an area of national importance in the early 1980s. It is an area of unique scenic beauty, flora and fauna, geological formations and cultural resources. On land, the park includes the three primary geological formations that make up the island. These rocks and their microclimates play an important role in supporting indigenous plants and wildlife. The limestone formation supports the island's largest natural freshwater spring, and formed the site of the agricultural settlements of the early Europeans.

War II. The Eagle refinery was closed down in the 1950s and the EXXON refinery in 1985 because of a worldwide glut in petroleum. The emphasis then turned to tourism.

In 1991 the Coastal Oil Company of Houston, Texas reopened the San Nicolas refinery, but the island has continued to invest heavily in tourism, which has long since replaced oil as Aruba's major industry. Some light industries produce tobacco, beverages and consumer goods but it is petroleum refining and tourism that give Aruba one of the highest standards of living in the Caribbean.

STATUS APARTE

Historically, Curaçao had long been the more senior of the ABC islands, a source of some resentment among Arubans who earned their own oil money but had to give it to the Netherlands Antilles Parliament in Curaçao. In the 1940s, a separation movement began, led by Gilberto François Croes, known locally as Bertico. After continuous lobbying the Dutch Government agreed to Aruba becoming autonomous in 1986. Though still within the Kingdom of the Netherlands (and dependent on the Netherlands for defence and foreign affairs) it now has its own currency and elected parliament.

The system of government in Aruba is based on Western democratic principles. A Governor is appointed by the Dutch monarch (presently Queen Beatrix) for a term of six years and acts as the sovereign's representative on the island. The unicameral national Legislature, the Staten, consists of a 21-member parliament, elected every four years. The Council of Ministers is presided over by the Prime Minister and forms the executive power.

In 1996 the Arubans were due to take full independence but, in the light of problems faced by like-minded islands in the Caribbean, these plans have been shelved indefinitely.

Opposite: *Richly coloured architecture is a striking feature in Oranjestad, Aruba's capital.*
Below: *Soft white sand carpets the beach beside the Tamarijn Beach Resort.*

LOCAL HIGHLIGHTS

Oranjestad, named after the reigning Royal Dutch House of Orange during the nineteenth century, is the capital city. It is a bustling free port town located on the south coast. Pastel-coloured Dutch colonial architecture is a notable feature, though many of the buildings in the Antillean style are actually modern and do not date from colonial times. The downtown area and the Seaport Village are the primary shopping areas.

Restored in 1980, the 17th-century Fort Zoutman is the oldest building in the country. The Willem (William) III Tower was added to the fort around 1868, serving as both town clock and lighthouse; its kerosene lamp was first lit on the birthday of King Willem III in 1869. The fortress now houses Aruba's Historical Museum, where Caiquetio Indian artefacts are displayed beside remnants of the Dutch colonial period and other items of local interest. Other museums include the Archaeological Museum at 1 Zoutmanstraat and the Numismatic Museum at 27 Zuidstraat.

Travelling northwest along the coast from Oranjestad's town centre, you pass the commercial area and reach Eagle Beach and the resort hotel area. Where the road turns north is 'De Olde Molen' restaurant, formerly an old windmill that was built in Holland in 1804 and then shipped to Aruba and reconstructed in 1960. Further north, beyond Palm Beach, Hadicurari is one of the most popular places for fast windsurfing. Here the water is shallow and there aren't any hotels to break up the wind.

The village of Noord has the Santa Anna Church, founded in 1766, rebuilt in 1831 and again in 1886; its present stone structure was erected in 1916. The church's neo-Gothic oak altar, pulpit and communion rails were made by the Dutch craftsman, Hendrik van der Geld, and prized at the Vatican Council exhibition in 1870. Not far from Noord is the Bubali Bird Sanctuary, where two man-made lakes attract more than 80 species of migratory birds.

Near the north coast is the tiny Chapel of Alto Vista, constructed on the site of a chapel built by the Spanish missionary, Domingo Antonio Silvester in 1750. It is so small that stone pews have been built in semi-circles outside the entrance of the Chapel. The Santa Anna Church and the Chapel of Alto Vista are still in use today, so visitors should dress appropriately.

Also on the north coast are the ruins of gold mines at Bushiribana, the centre of Aruba's gold rush during the nineteenth century and operational from 1872 to 1882. Nowadays the old gold smelter is often referred to as a Pirate Castle. A poorly maintained road then leads east on to a natural bridge, the largest of eight on the island. This coral formation 8m (25 feet) high and 30m (100 feet) long has been carved out by the pounding surf.

Inland, at Casibari and Ayó, there are huge diorite boulders that have been carved into unusual shapes by the

Opposite: *A well maintained walking trail leads through the dry surroundings of Aruba's Arikok National Park.*

wind. At Casibari steps lead up to the top for a good view of the island; Ayó has no steps so you have to scramble to the top, but it's worth the effort to see the Indian inscriptions marked on the boulders. Hooiberg (Mount Haystack), 165m (541ft) high, does have steps to the top, and on a clear day you can see across to the coast of Venezuela.

East of here is Arikok National Park, featuring some of the oldest Arawak frescoes, a restored old *cunucu* house and a great many of Aruba's plants and animals. Further east are the dunes and three caves of Boca Prins; nearby Fontein cave has a large chamber at the entrance and a 100m (110yd) tunnel containing Indian paintings. Further along the coast are the Guadirikiri caves, two large sunlit chambers connected by passages. A third cave, Huliba, is next to the 'Tunnel of Love'. Walking through the tunnel takes 30 minutes with a 10-minute return walk above ground. Helmets and torches can be hired for all the caves.

The road continues south to the second largest city in Aruba, San Nicolas, which started out as a company town for an oil refinery. It is the town that put Aruba on the map, since it is the birthplace of Aruba's Carnival, reputedly the third largest in the world after the carnivals of Rio and Trinidad. On Aruba's eastern point near Seroe Colorado, Grapefield Rock has been developed by Club Active Aruba for rock climbing; there is also some caving. Near Colorado Point Lighthouse there is a picturesque natural bridge.

Heading northwest back towards Oranjestad, you pass through Savaneta, the oldest town in Aruba and the original capital. This is where the Dutch first settled after re-establishing control of the island in 1816; today it is a fishing village. The oldest house in Aruba, a *cas de torto* or mud-hut dating back some 150 years, still stands here.

Further along the coast is Spanish Lagoon, once a pirates' hideout, now a bird sanctuary. There is quicksand so it is best not to walk off marked paths. Slightly inland is Frenchman's Pass, where the French attacked the Indians in 1700. From here you can head east to

Above: *The largest of Aruba's impressive natural bridges is near Andicuri on the north coast.*

Above: *Fish take refuge in the Arashi Airplane Wreck – formerly a twin-engined Beechcraft (Site 2).*
Below: *The engines still have their propellors attached at the Sonesta Airplane Wreck (Site 7)*

This site used to boast two aeroplanes. A Convair-400 (similar in shape to a Dakota DC-3), which was confiscated by the Aruban Government for drug smuggling, was sunk here through the collective efforts of some of Aruba's diving operators. It now sits upright in 15m (50ft) of water. The fore and aft doors and most of the interior were removed before it was sunk so the aircraft is easy to penetrate; and the propellers are still attached to the engines.

A twin-engined Beechcraft-18, which used to be in 5m (15ft) of water on top of the coral slope, has now disintegrated beyond recognition, though wreckage from both aircraft is spread around the seabed.

Straight out from Sonesta Beach Hotel's private island, the reef features elkhorn corals (*Acropora palmata*), staghorn corals (*Acropora cervicornis*), brain corals, fire corals and gorgonians. Barracuda, green moray eels and octopus are common among the fish life. The site begins around 5m (16ft) and the reef continues down to 30m (100ft).

The *Atlantis VI* submarine gets close to the aircraft so divers should keep a careful look-out when underwater. When surfacing it is safest to ascend the weighted line that is deployed by diving boats to a buoy off their stern.

8 SPONGE REEF
★★★

Location: South coast, off the south side of Sonesta Island at the western end
Access: By boat
Conditions: Normally calm
Average Depth: 12m (40ft)
Maximum Depth: 25m (80ft)
Visibility: 20m (65ft)
Often treated as a drift-dive as the current can be strong, this site begins at 5m (16ft) and has colourful orange elephant ear sponges (*Agelas clathrodes*), purple and yellow tube sponges, purple vase sponges, leaf and plate corals and gorgonians. Green moray eels, French angelfish, foureye butterflyfish and rock beauties are among the abundant fish life at this site, as well as lobsters and octopuses.

9 BARCADERA REEF
★★★★★

Location: South Coast, off the south side of the reef east of Sonesta Island
Access: By boat
Conditions: Normally calm
Average Depth: 15m (50ft)
Maximum Depth: 25m (80ft)
Visibility: 20m (65ft)

Beginning at 6m (20ft), this site is a healthy reef with elkhorn, staghorn and brain corals and large gorgonian sea fans on sand. Barracuda, mantas, wrasse, parrotfish, pufferfish and French angelfish have all been seen here.

10 KANTIL REEF
★★★

Location: South coast, off the south side of Sonesta Island, midway along (south of Bucuti Yacht Club)
Access: By boat
Conditions: Normally calm
Average Depth: 25m (80ft)
Maximum Depth: 33m (110ft)
Visibility: 25m (80ft)
There is a drop-off beginning at 12m (40ft) with large heads of brain, leaf, sheet and star coral and large gorgonian sea fans. The marine life includes manta rays, eagle rays, groupers, moray eels and the occasional sleeping nurse shark. This is a good dive for photographers.

11 SKALAHEIN
★★★

Location: South coast, off the southeast tip of Sonesta Island
Access: By boat
Conditions: Normally calm
Average Depth: 15m (50ft)
Maximum Depth: 30m+ (100ft+)
Visibility: 25m (80ft)
The reef slopes gently from 5m (15ft) to 15m (50ft), then more steeply past 30m (100ft). Known for its population of barracuda and the occasional manta ray or spotted eagle ray, it also has great coral formations and sponges. Brain and star corals dominate in shallow water and there are black corals and gorgonian sea fans below 20m (65ft). Seahorses have even been seen at this site, which is excellent for photography.

12 JANE SEA WRECK
★★★★

Location: South coast, off the south side of De Palm Island at the western end.
Access: By boat
Conditions: Normally calm, can be a very strong current
Average Depth: 25m (80ft)
Maximum Depth: 29m (95ft)
Visibility: 30m (100ft)
This spectacular wreck is a 75m (250ft) long freighter which was sunk intentionally as an artificial reef. It lies

*A*tlantis VI is a passenger-carrying submarine that has been taking tourists to dive sites off the coast of Aruba since 1990. US Coast Guard approved, it won the Aruba Tourism Scholarship Foundation (TOUSA) Iguana Award for the 'Most Outstanding Tourism Attraction'.

The vessel operates at normal atmospheric pressure, is air-conditioned, has 13 viewing windows, each 60cm (2ft) in diameter, and is electrically powered by DC batteries. She is 20m (65ft) long by 4m (13ft) beam and 6.4m (21ft) high, including the conning tower; displacement is 72,576kg (160,000lb). There is a crew of three and her passenger carrying capacity is 46. She has a submerged speed of 1¹/₂ knots.

GRACEFUL LADY OF THE DEEP

On the submarine voyage you can see an abundance of exotic fish and marine creatures, spectacular sponge gardens and remarkable formations. *Atlantis VI* also visits a number of dive sites that have fascinating histories. One of the particularly interesting sites is that of the *Mi Dushi*, known now as the Graceful Lady of the Deep. She is a wooden-hulled sailing trawler, built in 1928 and used in the North Sea until World War II, when she served as a cargo vessel and a rescue vessel for downed Allied aircrew. After the war finished the *Mi Dushi* was used for smuggling tobacco and whisky to Scandinavia. Eventually she was bought by a couple who converted her into one of Aruba's best-known charter boats. When the boat became too old for charters, she was cleaned of all fuel and oil and sunk as an environmentally friendly artificial reef.

After finishing the voyage on the *Atlantis VI*, you receive a certificate as proof that you have been to a depth of 150 feet. All trips depart from the dock located in the harbour opposite the Sonesta Resort in downtown Oranjestad. The submarine's dive site is a 30-minute ferry ride from the dock and the dive itself lasts for one hour. You can also book a place on the trip at Palm Beach, on the DePalm Pier across the beach from the Radisson Resort; group rates or special charters are available if booked in advance.

Below: *Typical of the kind of scenery visible from the Atlantis VI is this impressive brain coral.*

Above: *The Jane Sea Wreck is ablaze with colourful cup corals and encrusting sponges.*

upright with the 2m (6ft) propeller at 29m (95ft), the deck at 18m (60ft), the aft wheelhouse at 14m (45ft) and the bow at 15m (50ft). There is plenty of colour – orange cup corals, fire coral and red and pink encrusting sponges are found on the hull, and there are some black corals on her port side. The wreck attracts shoaling fish, barracuda, lobsters and green moray eels, while brain corals and gorgonian sea fans feature here.

In poor visibility, divers can find the ship's anchor chain at the bottom of the mooring rope and follow it in an arc to the right, first up the reef where there are large coral heads, then down the reef to the bow of the wreck. The superstructure and propeller are great for photography, as are the coral heads in shallow water where you can have a safety stop. There can be a very strong current.

PLONCO REEF
★★★

Location: South coast, off the south side of De Palm Island, midway along.
Access: By boat
Conditions: Normally calm
Average Depth: 20m (65ft)
Maximum Depth: 30m+ (100ft+)
Visibility: 30m (100ft)

Starting shallow at 6m (20ft), this reef slopes down beyond 30m (100ft) with large, healthy brain, fire and star corals, boring and encrusting sponges and gorgonians. Lobsters are common while fish life includes barracuda, rainbow runners (*Elagatis bipunnulata*), green moray eels and many species of reef fish.

There is often enough current to turn the dive into a drift dive. It is also a good dive for normal and macro photography.

DE PALM SLOPE
★★★★★★★★

Location: South coast, off the southeast end of De Palm Island
Access: Boat or shore
Conditions: Calm
Average Depth: 20m (65ft)
Maximum Depth: 36m (120ft)
Visibility: 25m (80ft)

This is a good shore dive from 5m (16ft) to deep water with fine coral formations and great snorkelling. Often done as a drift dive, there are barracuda, parrotfish, surgeonfish, yellowtail grunts and sergeant majors; spotted eagle rays are often seen.

CHINESE
Kowloon Restaurant
11 Emmastraat; tel 297 824950
Serves a mixture of favourite oriental dishes, with some more untraditional Chinese dishes.

FRENCH
Chez Mathilde
23 Havenstraat; tel 297 834968
Known as Aruba's most distinguished French restaurant. A 19th-century house kept in its original state, it has a reputation for seafood.

La Bouillabaisse
69 Bubali; tel 297 871408
Known for growing their own herbs. Specialises in traditional and authentic seafood, Caribbean and French cuisine.

DIVE FACILITIES
There are no facilities for Nitrox on Aruba. The Aruba Tourism Authority recommends the dive operators listed below that are marked with an asterisk.

Aruba Aqua Sports
Victor Hugostraat, Oranjestad; tel 297 823380; fax 297 833208
A small operator specializing in small groups for both boat and shore diving.

Aruba Scuba Center
1 Ade Musset Straat, Oranjestad; tel 297 821596; fax 297 821596
A small operator specializing in small groups for both boat and shore diving.

Dax Divers*
7 Kibaima, Santa Cruz; tel 297 851270; fax 297 867271
A small operator specializing in small groups for both boat and shore diving, with instruction up to Assistant Instructor level offered in Dutch, English and Spanish.

De Palm Watersports
tel 297 824545; fax 297 823012
A small operator specializing in small groups for both boat and shore diving.

Dive Aruba*
8 Williamsstraat, Oranjestad; tel 297 827337; fax 297 821817; e-mail: dbrand@centuryinter.net
A small operator offering boat dives for small groups and instruction up to PADI Divemaster in Dutch, English and Spanish.

Native Divers*
1 Koyari, Noord; tel 297 868763; fax 297 868515
A small operator that has been taking small groups diving for over twelve years. Boat and shore diving and instruction up to PADI Divemaster level in Dutch, English and Spanish.

Pelican Watersports*
P.O. Box 1194, 66 L.G. Smith Boulevard, Oranjestad (Pelican's jetty is beside the beach at Playa Linda Beach Resort);

tel 297 872302; fax 297 872315; e-mail: pelican-aruba@setarnet.aw
The second largest watersports/diving organization on Aruba with connections at Holiday Inn, La Cabana and Wyndham. Training up to Assistant Instructor level in Dutch, English, German and Spanish.

Pro Dive*
88 Ponton, Oranjestad; tel 297 825520; fax 297 877722
A small operator specializing in small groups. Boat and shore diving and instruction up to PADI Advanced Open Water level offered in Dutch, English and Spanish.

Red Sail Sports*
83 J.E.Irausquin Boulevard, Palm Beach; tel 297 861603, USA 800 255 6425; fax 297 866657; e-mail: info@redsail.com
The largest watersports/diving organization on Aruba and first Aruban diving operator to achieve the PADI 5-Star Dive Centre and Instructor Development Centre rating. Based at the Hyatt Regency Aruba Resort with connections at Allegro, Sonesta Resorts, Aruba Marriott Resort, Stauffer Hotel and Stellaris Casino. Well equipped to handle disabled divers, they also offer kayak diving. Instruction offered in Dutch, English, German, Portuguese, Spanish and Swedish.

Scuba Aruba
P.O. Box 4100 Noord; tel 297 834142; fax 297 875797; assang@curinfo.aw
A small operator specializing in small groups for both boat and shore diving.

S.E.A. Scuba*
P.O. Box 97, San Nicolas; tel 297 834877; fax 297 834875
A small operator specializing in small groups for both boat and shore diving.

Unique Watersports of Aruba*
79 J.E.Irausquin Boulevard (beside the beach at Aruba Palm Beach Resort); tel 297 823900; fax 297 860096; e-mail: uniquesports@setarnet.aw
The third largest watersports/diving organization in Aruba with connections at Aruba Palm Beach and The Mill. Instruction up to Divemaster level offered in Dutch, English, German, Portuguese and Spanish.

Atlantis Submarine; e-mail: goatlantis.com

FILM PROCESSING
Several laboratories offer 1-hour colour print processing and many resorts have pick-up points to collect exposed films and to return finished prints. However, there are no reliable E6 processing facilities.

Artphoto
26D Jaburibari, tel 297 838980
De La Salle Straat, tel 297 832320
21 Helfrich Straat, San Nicolas, tel 297 845220
Checkpoint Color 1 Hour Labs
10 Columbusstraat, tel 297 822284

K & H Photolab Services NV
82 L.G. Smith Boulevard, tel 297 8311331
Playa Linda One Hour Photo
87 J.E. Irausquin Boulevard, tel 297 866202
Poly Color Prints NV
16 Schotlandstraat, tel 297 836760

EMERGENCIES
There is no recompression chamber on the island. The nearest is on Curaçao and patients who require hyperbaric treatment are transferred by low-flying aircraft.

Hotels have doctors and dentists on call. The Dr Horacio Oduber Hospital has reputable medical staff and is equipped with up-to-date equipment. It is located across from Eagle Beach on L.G Smith Boulevard, near to the main hotel area. Services such as oxygen and haemodialysis are available. For more information contact:

Dr Horacio Oduber Hospital
Sasakiweg, Aruba; tel 297 874300; fax 297 873348

Aruba Emergency Telephone Numbers:
All Emergencies	115
Police	100
Fire	115
Ambulance Oranjestad	821234
Ambulance San Nicolas	845050
Hospital	874300

USEFUL CONTACTS
Visit the Aruba web site: http://www.interknowledge.com/aruba

ATA – Aruba and Caribbean
PO Box 1019, 172 L.G. Smith Boulevard, Orangestad, Aruba; tel 297 823777; fax 297 834702; e-mail: ata.aruba@toaruba.com

Aruba Tourism Authority (ATA) – Europe
1 Schimmelpennincklaan, 2517 JN, The Haag, Holland; tel 31 70 3 566220; fax 31 70 3 604877; e-mail: ata.europe@toaruba.com

ATA – Chicago
401 Wilmette Avenue, Westmont, Illinois 60559; tel 630 663 1363; fax 630 663 1362; e-mail: ata.chicago@toaruba.com

ATA – Florida
Greater Miami Office, One Financial Plaza, Suite 136, Fort Lauderdale, Florida 33394; tel 954 767 6477; fax 954 767 0432; e-mail: ata.florida@toaruba.com

ATA – Canada
86 Bloor Street West, Suite 204, Toronto, Ontario, M5S 1M5, Canada; tel 416 975 1950; 800 268 3042; fax 416 975 1947; e-mail: ata.canada@toaruba.com

Dirección de Turismo de Aruba – Venezuela
Centro Ciudad Comercial Tamanaco, Torre C. Piso 8, Oficina C-805, Chuao, Caracas, Venezuela; tel 582 959 1256; fax 582 959 6346; e-mail: aruba01@ibm.net

BONAIRE

Over the last twenty years, Bonaire has developed a reputation as one of the best diving and snorkelling destinations in the Caribbean, mainly as a result of the island's conservation of its marine resources with the creation of a national marine park. The license plates proclaiming 'Diver's Paradise' are a testament to how important diving is to the locals. There are also many other activities to enjoy, including mountain biking, horseback riding, windsurfing, sea kayaking, deep-sea fishing and caving – over the last ten years more than 40 caves have been discovered. You can charter a yacht, take a trip on a glass-bottomed boat, go bird watching, see Indian frescoes, gamble at a casino or enjoy a day trip to Venezuela.

Bonaire is not known for its beaches since the sand tends to be full of broken coral and hard on the feet. The beaches on the leeward coast are narrow, though those in front of some hotels have been improved with extra sand. However, they do offer tranquillity and there are no hawkers. There are no high rise hotels or traffic lights on Bonaire, and jet skis are supposed to be banned (though you may see them racing about at dusk).

HISTORY
Bonaire's earliest known inhabitants were the Caiquetios, who came from Venezuela around 1000 AD. The Arawak Indian name for the island, Bo-nah, means low country, and later became 'Boynay' in the local dialect.

Alonso de Ojeda and Amerigo Vespucci claimed Bonaire for Spain in 1499 and named it Isla de Brazil, which means Island of Dyewood, since the dye the Caiquetios used in their cave paintings came from the dyewood tree. As Bonaire had neither gold nor enough rainfall for large-scale agricultural use, the Spanish saw no reason to develop the colony. They forced the native Caiquetios into slavery and deported them to work on the plantations and mines of Hispaniola. As a result the native population was almost eradicated by 1515.

In 1526, Juan de Ampues, the governor of Aruba, Bonaire, and Curaçao, began cattle ranching on the island. Using Caiquetios and other Indians from Venezuela as labourers, he soon had cows, sheep, goats, pigs, donkeys and horses being raised. The animals' hides were

---

Opposite: *The varied scenery of Washington-Slagbaai National Park includes limestone headlands.*
Above: *On mainland Bonaire most dive sites are clearly marked from the shore.*

WASHINGTON-SLAGBAAI NATIONAL PARK

Over a century ago, two plantations, or *kunukus* in Papiamento, called Washington and Slagbaai, occupied the site of this national park. They exported cattle, goats, aloe, charcoal and salt, each plantation from its own harbour. A park was first established in 1969 from the land that had been Washington plantation. Then in 1979 Slagbaai (the name means slaughter because cattle were slaughtered here) was added to form the present-day park. You can still discern the fence that separated the two properties.

The 5463ha (13,500-acre) Washington-Slagbaai National Park presents a cross-section of the landscape, flora and fauna of the island. Covering nearly one-fifth of Bonaire, it offers arid desert scenery, salt pans, hills and beaches. The animal life includes iguanas, wild donkeys and goats. There are two rugged but driveable dirt roads through the park, though four-wheel drive vehicles are recommended.

The park is open daily from 0800 to 1700 except on official holidays, though no entry is permitted after 15:00. Entry is US$5 per person.

worth more than their meat, so they required little tending and were generally let loose to wander freely. Today the island has abundant feral populations of donkeys and goats.

For the next three centuries, few of the island's inhabitants arrived willingly. There was an inland settlement at Rincon, away from pirate raids, but development was not encouraged. Bonaire's immigrants were mostly convicts from Spanish colonies in South America. The Dutch admiral Boudewijn Hendricksz landed Spanish and Portuguese prisoners to establish the town of Antriol and for most of the next 300 years, Bonaire remained a penal colony.

In 1633, the Dutch captured the ABC islands. Curaçao became a naval base in their war with Spain, while Bonaire became a plantation of the Dutch West India Company. The remaining convicts, Indians and a few African slaves were put to work cultivating dyewood and maize and, from 1639, collecting salt dried by the sun. Slave quarters, no taller than 1.2m (4ft) and built of stone, can still be found around Rincon and along the saltpans as a grim reminder of Bonaire's history.

When the Dutch West India Company collapsed in 1791, the Dutch government confiscated its property. The slaves, now owned by the Kingdom of the Netherlands, came to be known as 'government slaves'. The slaves were allowed to grow and sell their own produce, and sometimes even to

rich reef that harbours shoals of algae-grazing blue tangs. Yellow and green tube sponges are common and turtles are often sighted.

11 OL' BLUE
★★★★★★★★★

Location: West coast, off Boca di Toto
Access: By boat or shore
Conditions: Light to moderate currents
Average Depth: 20m (65ft)
Maximum Depth: 45m (150ft)
Visibility: 30m (100ft)
Ol' Blue is named after the rich blue colour of the sea that is found over the site's shallows. The dive is similar to Weber's Joy (Site 15), but has even more fish. A shelf at 6m (20ft) extends seaward for 90m (100yd), covered with staghorn coral, gorgonian sea fans, sea plumes and sea rods, star coral, sponges and a rich fish life. The drop-off starts at 10m (33ft) and descends to sand. At the eastern end, various fish shelter around several large boulders including bigeyes, French angelfish, grunts, tiger groupers, mahogany snappers, scorpionfish, barracuda and shoals of horse-eye jacks.

12 COUNTRY GARDEN
★★★★

Location: West coast, off the southeast of Boca di Toto
Access: By boat
Conditions: Moderate currents
Average Depth: 20m (65ft)
Maximum Depth: 40m (130ft)
Visibility: 30m (100ft)
At this site, large boulders that have fallen from the cliffs provide shelter for schoolmaster snappers, grunts, bigeyes, soldierfish, squirrelfish and goatfish.

13 BON BINI NA CAS
★★★★

Location: West coast, west of 1000 Steps
Access: By boat or by shore by swimming from 1000 Steps
Conditions: Normally calm
Average Depth: 20m (65ft)
Maximum Depth: 40m (130ft)
Visibility: 30m (100ft)

Below: *The conspicuous markings of the flamingo tongue are instantly recognisable.*

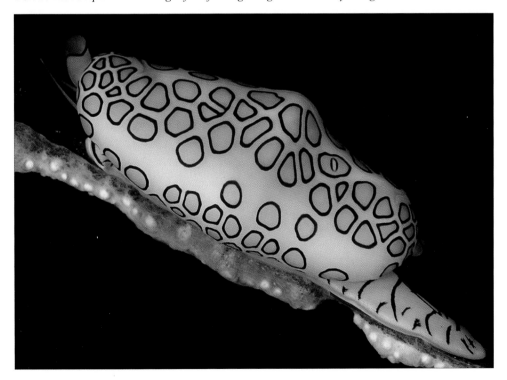

Above: *A diver explores the reef, with its light covering of encrusting sponges and cup corals.*
Below: *Healthy staghorn coral is a common sight on Bonaire's reefs.*

The profile of this site is similar to that of Andrea II (Site 19), with a gentle slope to 15m (50ft) then a drop-off.

PETRIE'S PILLAR
★★★★

Location: West coast, southeast of Andrea I
Access: By boat or shore
Conditions: Normally calm
Average Depth: 20m (65ft)
Maximum Depth: 35m (115ft)
Visibility: 30m (100ft)
Petrie's Pillar is a dive for novices. It is named after a friend of Captain Don Stewart and the pillar coral that grows on the reef. The terrain is similar to that of Andrea I and II (sites 19-20). The shallows also host shoals of blue tangs.

SMALL WALL
★★★★★★★★

Location: West coast, opposite the Black Durgon Inn.
Access: By boat or shore; permission is needed to cross the private property for shore entry.
Conditions: Normally calm
Average Depth: 20m (65ft)
Maximum Depth: 40m (120ft)
Visibility: 30m (100ft)
A shallow, well-protected wall dive that is ideal for beginners and night dives. The top of the reef has elkhorn and brain coral and lots of branching gorgonians that seahorses attach themselves to. Parrotfish, bigeyes, soldierfish, squirrelfish, grunts and French angelfish abound. A small wall starts 30m (100ft) out from the shore and drops from 12m (40ft) to 22m (70ft). A cave can be found at 18m (60ft), and there is a possibility of seeing a sleeping nurse shark or green moray eels. Below the cave, large elephant ear sponges make this a good site for underwater photography. Lobsters can be found on night dives.

CLIFF
★★★★★★★★

Location: West coast, opposite the Hamlet Villas north of Captain Don's Habitat.
Access: By boat or shore
Conditions: Normally calm
Average Depth: 20m (65ft)
Maximum Depth: 40m (130ft)
Visibility: 30m (100ft)

A channel runs through elkhorn coral into a shelf with gorgonians and stony corals. The drop-off descends as a short wall from 9m (30ft) to 22m (70ft) with a ledge of sand 2m (6ft) wide then slopes to sand at 40m (130ft). The wall has orange and tube sponges, gorgonian sea whips and abundant fish life. There is supposed to be an underwater stone memorial from Captain Don to 'divers who have gone before us', marked with a plaque and dive flag, but I didn't ever come across it!

LA MACHACA
★★★★★★★★★

Location: West coast, off Captain Don's Habitat
Access: From the shore
Conditions: Normally calm
Average Depth: 14m (45ft)
Maximum Depth: 40m (130ft)
Visibility: 30m (100ft)
Captain Don's Habitat's house reef, this site is named after the wreck of a local 14m (45ft) fishing boat *La Machaca*, 30m (100ft) from the shore in 14m (45ft) of water. Ideal for training divers, snorkelling, night diving and general fish photography, most of the reef fish encountered on Bonaire can be found here. Because of the popularity of this site much of the marine life has become so used to divers that you can find yourself being aproached by fish (it seems that only drums are shy). Lizardfish and peacock flounders (*Bothus lunatus*) are common and spotted moray eels can even be found swimming freely during daylight.

A rope stretched along the seabed from the shore-entry jetty (Baby Dock) goes directly out 15m (50ft) to the drop-off and then down the slope to another deeper wreck. Divers returning to the jetty can easily

---

BONAIRE GUIDED SNORKELLING PROGRAM

A group of expert snorkellers and underwater photographers together with the marine park authorities and local operators researched the leeward coast of the main island and the coast of Klein Bonaire to set up the Bonaire Guided Snorkelling Program.

There are 12 sites in the program, each selected to offer distinct experiences. However, remember that many other excellent snorkelling sites may also be found, especially immediately adjacent to those listed. Where a site is marked with an asterisk, the snorkel site lies inshore of the dive site.

Bonaire sites	Klein Bonaire sites
Playa Funchi	No Name*
Nukove	Leonora's Reef
1000 Steps	Jerry's Jam*
Cliff	Munk's Haven*
Windsock	Just A Nice Dive*
Invisibles	
Mangroves	

locate this rope to find their way back without straying into the path of boats leaving from or returning to the separate boat jetty (Papa Dock).

There are elkhorn coral, palometa and flounders in the shallow water by the entry jetty, brain and star coral, gorgonians, orange elephant ear and tube sponges over the drop-off, and the wrecks attract tarpon, jacks, grunts, snappers, sergeant majors and groupers.

25 REEF SCIENTIFICO
★★★★★★★★

Location: West coast, southeast of Captain Don's Habitat
Access: From the shore
Conditions: Normally calm
Average Depth: 12m (40ft)
Maximum Depth: 40m (130ft)
Visibility: 30m (100ft)
South of La Machaca (Site 24), a transect (grid system) has been set out in 12m (40ft) of water to monitor algal growth on the reef. The site is much the same as La Machaca but fewer divers have been here so the fish are not as tame.

26 BUDDY'S REEF
★★★★★★★★

Location: West coast, in front of Buddy Dive Resort
Access: From the shore
Conditions: normally calm
Average Depth: 20m (65ft)
Maximum Depth: 40m (130ft)
Visibility: 30m (100ft)
This shore dive is great for beginners and snorkellers, with mild currents. Black crinoids perch on coral heads in the shallows; night divers often encounter a shoal of tarpon.

27 BARI REEF
★★★★★★

Location: West coast, in front of Sand Dollar Condominium Resort
Access: From the shore
Conditions: Moderate currents
Average Depth: 20m (65ft)
Maximum Depth: 37m (120ft)
Visibility: 30m (100ft)

Above: *Kralendijk's Town Pier (Site 30) is the best known of Bonaire's dive sites.*
Opposite: *An adult stoplight parrotfish grazes on algae using its large parrot-like beak.*

Sand Dollar Resort's house reef, this site is ideal for snorkelling and training novice divers though it is showing signs of wear. There is usually some current, so start your dive by heading into it. A flat, sandy plateau continues out 91m (100yd) from the service deck to the drop-off, which varies in depth from 6m (20ft) to 12m (40ft). The plateau and the drop-off have star corals, gorgonians and sponges, and attract French angelfish, foureye butterflyfish, trunkfish, peacock flounders, scorpionfish, bigeyes, soldierfish, squirrelfish and goatfish. Night divers regularly encounter tarpon (*Megalops atlanticus*).

28 FRONT PORCH
★★★★★★★★

Location: West coast, in front of the Sunset Beach Resort
Access: From the shore
Conditions: Light to moderate currents
Average Depth: 20m (65ft)
Maximum Depth: 30m (100ft)
Visibility: 30m (100ft)

Accessed from either the dive jetty or the beach, Front Porch is an easy dive ideal for diver training or snorkelling. Beginning at 5m (16ft) under the pier, the slope continues down to beyond 25m (80ft), where a small wreck of a tugboat lies upside down. The wreck is covered in orange *Tubastrea* cup coral and harbours a profuse fish life.

29 SOMETHING SPECIAL
★★★★★★

Location: West coast, just south of Kralendijk Marina entrance
Access: By boat or shore
Conditions: Mild currents
Average Depth: 20m (65ft)
Maximum Depth: 40m (130ft)
Visibility: 20m (65ft)

This is an area where sailing boats are allowed to anchor. There is very little coral growth here but there is abundant fish life; rays can often be seen at the sandy bottom. Good for night diving.

DECEPTIVE CORALS

Many divers are surprised when they first see black coral underwater, since it is not in fact black at all. The polyps of most black corals are translucent with pigments that make the colony appear brown, green or grey – although in wire corals they are a brighter red or yellow-green. As in stony corals, black coral polyps have six tentacles but ,unlike stony corals, they are not retractable.

It is only the skeleton of black coral that is black. This material is laid down in concentric layers; if the skeleton is cut crosswise it looks like the yearly growth rings of trees. In deep water some black corals grow very large, and it is the branches of these that are collected so that the skeleton can be fashioned into jewellery.

The scientific name for black coral, antipatharian, means anti-disease, a reference to a historical belief in its medicinal properties. Due to their collection for jewellery some black coral forests have disappeared from the Caribbean – you can protect the remaining black coral trees by not purchasing products made from them.

Black corals are protected under the Convention in International Trade in Endangered Species (CITES) – they cannot be exported or imported except under licence.

---

30 TOWN PIER
★★★★

Location: West coast, off the Town (North) Pier, next to the customs office in Kralendijk
Access: By boat or shore (with permission)
Conditions: Normally calm
Average Depth: 5m (16ft)
Maximum Depth: 9m (30ft)
Visibility: 20m (65ft)

This is the best known dive site on Bonaire and one of the best night dive sites in the world. In 9m (30ft) of water, the pier's stanchions are home to a rich world of small invertebrate life and lots of other marine creatures seeking shelter or food. There are usually a couple of large tugboats coming and going, and permission should first be obtained from the harbour master to be sure that no large ships are expected that could pose a danger to divers (also the visibility can be lowered to just a few metres by the movement of large ships). You should be accompanied by a local dive guide and must be careful about where you surface, or you could become trapped between the pier and any boats docking against it. At night, aim for your dive boat's location beacon.

Boat diving is almost always done at night with one of the island's dive operators. When shore diving you should enter and exit the water by the steps down to the small beach that is immediately south of the pier. Walk the few metres to the pier and you can then duck safely under it in water that is too shallow for large boats.

The pier begins at a right angle from the shore and then turns north at a right angle. Its stanchions are covered in sponges of many colours including orange, yellow, green and purple. The site is a macro photographer's paradise, featuring orange *Tubastrea* cup corals, seahorses, Christmas tree worms, arrow and decorator crabs and various shrimps. The shelter of the pier acts as a nursery for juvenile fish including frogfish, French angelfish, foureye and banded butterflyfish, trunkfish, pufferfish, moray eels and shoals of bluestriped and smallmouth grunts (*Haemulon scirius* and *H. chrysargyreum*). It is well worth searching among the tyres and other rubbish strewn around the seafloor as many juveniles (including lobsters, octopuses, chain moray eels [*Gymnothorax moringa*], drums and soapfish) find shelter there.

31 CALABAS REEF
★★★★★★★★

Location: West coast, in front of Dive Bonaire at the Divi Flamingo Resort and the Carib Inn.
Access: Any of Dive Bonaire's jetties or the Carib Inn jetty
Conditions: Mild currents
Average Depth: 30m (65ft)
Maximum Depth: 27m (90ft)
Visibility: 30m (100ft)

This site is fine for snorkellers and all levels of divers, from novice to advanced. It begins as a shallow sandy shelf with some staghorn and star coral, anemones and sponges and many reef fish including French angelfish, parrotfish, snappers, bigeyes, soldierfish, squirrelfish Creole wrasse and Spanish hogfish.

The drop-off starts at 9m (30ft) and slopes down to 27m (90ft) and includes orange sponges, purple tube sponges, star coral, most species of reef fish and the occasional turtle or ray. Off the Calabas Restaurant jetty there is an anchor at 9m (25ft) and just below this there is an old lifeboat.

32 EIGHTEEN PALMS
★★★★★★★★

Location: West coast, opposite The Lieutenant Governor's House
Access: By boat or shore
Conditions: Mild currents
Average Depth: 20m (65ft)
Maximum Depth: 30m (100ft)
Visibility: 30m (100ft)

Opposite: *Sponges, like this orange rope sponge, are supported by a skeleton of spicules and fibres.*

system relied on the fact that red is the first colour of light to be filtered out by water with depth; when the red ribbons appeared to look black the divers knew that they were diving too deep.

In 1972 Captain Don set up Aquaventure, one of the first dedicated diving companies in the Caribbean. It was not until 1976, however, that he opened Captain Don's Habitat. In these early days, not only was Captain Don the dive guide and resort manager, but also the head cook, bottle washer, plumber, electrician and gardener! A large part of the Habitat was used as a nursery for local plants, as Captain Don was keen to promote not just marine conservation but also conservation on land. The ethos behind the Habitat was to encourage 'total diving freedom' – and to learn and care for all ecological systems.

CONSERVATION TO THE FORE

Even in these early days of diving, Captain Don realised that diving and spear fishing were causing a great deal of harm to Bonaire's reef system. If the reef system were to have a future it had to have a programme of conservation. Captain Don therefore lobbied hard to preserve Bonaire's underwater resources, and became instrumental in setting up the Bonaire Marine Park. One of Captain Don's ideas was to initiate the permanent mooring programme, where permanent moorings marked by buoys are set up to protect the delicate reef system. He also put forward the plan to temporarily close certain busy dive sites every now and then to allow them to 'rest' and regain their natural splendour.

Captain Don was keen to spread the idea of conservation and encouraged other Caribbean islands to follow the example Bonaire had set in preserving its reef system. In 1977 he co-founded the Caribbean Underwater Resort Operators (CURO), which brought together the operators of 18 Caribbean islands to encourage marine conservation throughout the Caribbean.

In 1987 Captain Don sold the Habitat, becoming a minority shareholder. Still very active, he now has a farm growing local plants, Island Grower N.V., and a landscape gardening business. Captain Don has been showered with recognition for his contributions to diving, to conservation and to Bonaire. On January 30th 1998, at DEMA (the Diving Equipment and Marketing Association's annual trade show), Captain Don was presented with the 'DEMA Reaching Out Award', one of the highest honours in the diving industry. This award puts Captain Don in the hall of fame with previous winners that include Captain Jacques-Yves Cousteau, Hans Hass, Jean-Michel Cousteau, Dr Eugenie Clark, Stan Waterman and Sylvia Earle.

When Captain Don started out on his pioneering road to conservation, his efforts were often regarded as rather controversial and somewhat unorthodox. Now he and Bonaire are considered to be world leaders in the modern drive towards preserving the environment for future generations to enjoy. As he says, 'Bonaire is to reef ecology as Greenwich is to time.'

South Bonaire

38 PUNT VIERKANT
★★★★

Location: West coast, south of Punk Vierkant lighthouse, north of the Transworld Radio transmitting pylons
Access: By boat or shore
Conditions: Mild currents
Average Depth: 20m (65ft)
Maximum Depth: 30m (100ft)
Visibility: 30m (100ft)
This site marks the start of the double-reef system, part of the 'Alice in Wonderland' complex (see Site 42). Staghorn coral and gorgonians can be seen in the shallows, while the reef slope has large brain and star corals, sponges and gorgonians down to a channel of sand between the two reefs at 22–30m (70–100ft). There are scrawled filefish, Spanish hogfish, trunkfish, bigeyes, soldierfish, squirrelfish and rock beauties. The outer reef attracts barracuda, snappers, jacks, groupers and rays.

39 THE LAKE
★★★★

Location: West coast, southwest of the Transworld Radio transmitting pylons
Access: By boat or shore
Conditions: Mild currents
Average Depth: 20m (65ft)
Maximum Depth: 30m (100ft)
Visibility: 30m (100ft)

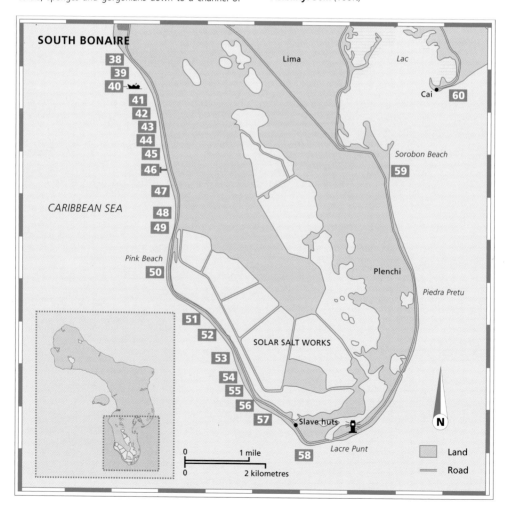

SOUTH BONAIRE

38
39
40
41
42
43
44
45
46
47
48
49

CARIBBEAN SEA

Pink Beach
50

51
52
53
54
55
56
57
58

SOLAR SALT WORKS

Slave huts

Lacre Punt

Lima

Lac

Cai
60

Sorobon Beach
59

Plenchi

Piedra Pretu

N

0   1 mile
0   2 kilometres

Land
Road

This is another double-reef dive, part of the 'Alice in Wonderland' complex. The Lake features gorgonian sea rods, sea whips and sea plumes, purple tube sponges, stony corals and a profusion of reef fish, including filefish, Spanish hogfish, trunkfish, bigeyes, soldierfish, squirrelfish and rock beauties. The seaward side of the outer reef has barracuda, snappers, jacks and groupers.

40 HILMA HOOKER
★★★

Location: West coast, south of The Lake (Site 39)
Access: By boat or shore
Conditions: Strong currents
Average Depth: 25m (80ft)
Maximum Depth: 30m (100ft)
Visibility: 20m (65ft)

The 72m (235ft), 1043-tonne (1027-ton) Korean freighter *Hilma Hooker* docked at the Town Pier for urgent repairs but alert Customs officers found marijuana hidden on board so the ship was confiscated and the drug burnt. As she was slowly sinking, on September 12th 1984 Bonaire's dive operators towed her out to the sand between the double-reef system and deliberately sunk her.

Unfortunately the anti-fouling wasn't removed so marine organisms have been slow to establish themselves on the structure. However, it is now being colonized by sponges and is shelter to tiger and black groupers, black margates (*Anisotremus surilnamensis*), mahogany snappers and yellowtail snappers (*Ocyurus chrysurus*). Large horse-eye jacks cruise the open water beyond the wreck and midnight parrotfish can be seen grazing on the hull. Except where there are large open compartments in the central section, penetration of the wreck is not advised.

A cluster of dive-buoys along the wreck now marks the site. The ship rests on her starboard side at the bottom of the reef slope – the highest point of the vessel is at 18m (60ft).

41 ANGEL CITY
★★★★

Location: West coast, south of the Hilma Hooker (Site 40)
Access: By boat or shore
Conditions: Moderate currents
Average Depth: 25m (80ft)
Maximum Depth: 30m (100ft)
Visibility: 20m (65ft)

Another double-reef dive, this site is named after its friendly angelfish, which approach divers. There is a 'swim-through' coral arch near to the mooring, which provides a frame for photography. The outer reef has large boulders and large heads of star coral.

PUFFERFISH TETRODOTOXIN

Pufferfish are extremely dangerous to eat and lead to some 30 deaths each year in Japan, where the fish is eaten in restaurants as a delicacy. The livers and ovaries of pufferfish contain Tetrodotoxin, an anaesthetic 160,000 times more potent than cocaine and 500 times stronger than cyanide.

Pufferfish extract is used for voodoo in Haiti, where there are well documented cases of people appearing to be dead and victims only recovering after burial. Recovery is natural but slow.

Taken in tiny quantities, however, the toxin can cut down cravings in the brain by calming signals in the hypothalamus, the section of the brain that co-ordinates the senses and controls feelings of addiction. This has led to a Canadian pharmaceutical company incorporating it in a drug called Tetrodin, which is undergoing trials as a pain killer.

42 ALICE IN WONDERLAND
★★★★

Location: West coast, south of Angel City (Site 41)
Access: By boat or shore
Conditions: Moderate currents
Average Depth: 25m (80ft)
Maximum Depth: 30m (100ft)
Visibility: 20m (67ft)

This site lies roughly midway along the double-reef system (which also includes sites 38–49). The two distinct reefs are separated by a sand channel where garden eels and stingrays can be seen. There are staghorn corals and gorgonians in the shallows as well as French angelfish and parrotfish. The slope drops from 12m (40ft) to the sand at 25–30m (80–100ft) and the swim across the sand to the second reef is about 20m (65ft). This second reef rises to within 15m (50ft) of the surface and then drops off again into deep water where there is brain and star coral and shoals of black margate and schoolmaster snappers.

43 AQUARIUS
★★★★

Location: West coast, south of Alice in Wonderland (Site 42)
Access: By boat or shore
Conditions: Moderate currents
Average Depth: 25m (80ft)
Maximum Depth: 30m (100ft)
Visibility: 20m (65ft)

An easy dive that is part of the double reef system. Parrotfish, angelfish, surgeonfish and butterflyfish can be found between the two reefs. There are staghorn corals and gorgonians, jacks, grunts, trunkfish, bigeyes, soldierfish, squirrelfish and groupers. You may also spot rays or turtles in the shallows. On the seaward side of the outer reef you will encounter barracuda and large groupers.

Above: *A diver is dwarfed by the imposing stern section of the Hilma Hooker (Site 40).*
Opposite: *Salt Pier (Site 46) is home to a wide variety of fish, including French angelfish.*

44 LARRY'S LAIR
★★★★

Location: West coast, south of Aquarius (Site 43), the second dive site north of Salt Pier
Access: By boat or shore
Conditions: Moderate currents
Average Depth: 25m (80ft)
Maximum Depth: 30m (100ft)
Visibility: 20m (65ft)
The shore entry is over sharp rocks so hard-soled booties are recommended; this and the current make shore entry more difficult than that by boat. Still part of the double reef system, the topography is similar to that of Aquarius. Staghorn and star corals, gorgonians, Spanish hogfish, trunkfish, bigeyes, soldierfish, squirrelfish and rock beauties are found in the shallow water, while the outer reef attracts barracuda, snappers, jacks and groupers.

45 JEANNE'S GLORY
★★★★

Location: West coast, north of Salt Pier (Site 46)
Access: By boat or shore
Conditions: Moderate currents
Average Depth: 25m (80ft)
Maximum Depth: 30m (100ft)
Visibility: 20m (65ft)
Some operators and maps refer to this site as Jeannie's Glory. Still part of the double reef system with similar topography, this is another easy dive with lots of gorgonians in the shallows and sandy bottom for rays. Staghorn and star corals, angelfish, butterflyfish, trumpetfish, goatfish, snappers, Spanish hogfish, trunkfish, bigeyes, soldierfish and squirrelfish are common in the shallow water, while the outer reef has barracuda, snappers, jacks and groupers. Turtles are often seen along these southern dive sites.

46 SALT PIER
★★★★

Location: West coast, opposite the salt loading pier at the end of the overhead conveyor belt of the Salt Works
Access: From the shore
Conditions: Light currents
Average Depth: 15m (50ft)
Maximum Depth: 15m (50ft)
Visibility: 20m (65ft)

This site should not be attempted when a ship is loading its cargo or arriving or departing from the pier. As with the Town Pier (Site 30), the stanchions are covered with coral and sponge growth and act as shelter for juvenile fish. The stanchions near to the shore are in 6m (20ft) of water while those further out are in 15m (50ft). The drop-off slopes into deep water but it is the area directly beneath the pier that is more interesting. The pier itself is T-shaped; the stem of the 'T' runs west at right angles to the shore and the top of the 'T' runs north–south.

Tubastrea cup corals are a blaze of colour at night and there are tiny crabs, shrimps and fish among the growth on the stanchions. Surgeonfish graze the algae and French and queen angelfish, drums, soapfish, pufferfish, snappers, grunts, moray eels, groupers and shoals of goatfish and Creole wrasse are abundant. A great dive for photography.

47 SALT CITY
★★★★

Location: West coast, south of the salt loading pier of the Salt Works
Access: By boat or shore
Conditions: Moderate currents
Average Depth: 25m (80ft)
Maximum Depth: 30m (100ft)
Visibility: 20m (65ft)

Part of the double-reef system, Salt City features elkhorn, fire, staghorn and star corals, French angelfish, palometa, groupers, snappers, sand tilefish, garden eels, and occasionally eagle rays and turtles.

48 TORI'S REEF
★★★★★★★★

Location: West coast, by the outflow from the Salt Works
Access: By boat or shore
Conditions: Moderate currents
Average Depth: 25m (80ft)
Maximum Depth: 30m (100ft)
Visibility: 25m (80ft)

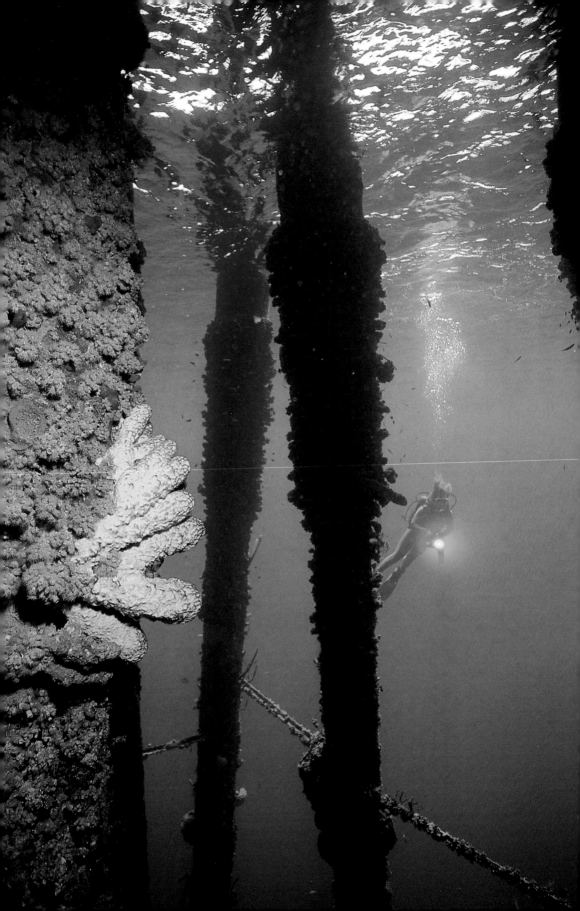

69 SHARON'S SERENITY

★★★★★★★★

Location: West coast of Klein Bonaire, southwest of Valerie's Hill (Site 68), near the lighthouse
Access: By boat
Conditions: Medium currents
Average Depth: 20m (65ft)
Maximum Depth: 40m (130ft)
Visibility: 30m (100ft)

The currents here can be a problem but are not as strong as those at Munks Haven or Southwest Corner (sites 71–72). Elkhorn, staghorn and star corals and prolific growth of gorgonian sea fans, sea rods, sea whips and sea plumes mark the shallow shelf, which extends offshore for 45m (150ft). Beginning at 12m (40ft), the drop-off descends into deep water. Equally rich in growth, the drop-off has undercut star corals forming a mushroom-like effect. Harbouring many species of fish, there are large jewfish, while barracuda and groupers are seen at cleaning stations. whitespotted filefish, parrotfish, black durgon, French angelfish, banded and foureye butterflyfish, cowfish and trumpetfish are regularly sighted. Basket stars are found on this side of Klein Bonaire on night dives.

70 TWIXT

★★★★★★★★

Location: West coast of Klein Bonaire, southwest of Sharon's Serenity (Site 69)
Access: By boat
Conditions: Medium currents
Average Depth: 20m (65ft)
Maximum Depth: 40m (130ft)
Visibility: 30m (100ft)

The dive sites around the southwest corner of Klein Bonaire are among the best in the Caribbean. Similar to Munk's Haven (Site 71), Twixt features large basket sponges, gorgonian sea fans, sea rods and sea whips, black coral, tube sponges, star corals and cleaning stations. The coral wall slopes down to a sandy bottom.

Below: *A nocturnal predator, the schoolmaster snapper may hang around singly by day.*

71 MUNK'S HAVEN
★★★★

Location: Southwest coast of Klein Bonaire, north of Southwest Corner (Site 72)
Access: By boat
Conditions: Moderate to strong currents
Average Depth: 20m (65ft)
Maximum Depth: 40m (130ft)
Visibility: 30m (100ft)

Named after Illinois dive shop-owner Elmer Munk, who was a regular visitor, Munk's Haven is one of the best dives in the Caribbean. There are copious quantities of staghorn and star coral interspersed with lush gorgonian growth in the shallows. The drop-off slopes steeply from 12m (40ft), where there are large sculptured coral heads, down to sand at 37m (120ft). Vase and orange elephant ear sponges, brain and star corals are common on the face of the slope, and there is a multitude of fish species including large groupers at cleaning stations.

72 SOUTHWEST CORNER
★★★★

Location: The southwest corner of Klein Bonaire
Access: By boat
Conditions: Moderate to strong currents
Average Depth: 20m (65ft)
Maximum Depth: 37m (120ft)
Visibility: 40m (130ft)

Another of the best dives in the Caribbean, this is a particular favourite with those who teach underwater photography. Southwest Corner has great visibility and appears to have thicker staghorn corals in the shallows and taller star corals and gorgonians along the drop-off than elsewhere. Large tiger and yellowmouth groupers (*Mycteroperca tigris* and *M. interstitialis*) are found at cleaning stations, black durgons; golden coneys (*Cephalopholis fulvus*), scrawled and whitespotted filefish, French and queen angelfish, sergeant majors, grunts, pufferfish, bigeyes, soldierfish, squirrelfish and yellowtail snappers are common, and shoals of blue tangs graze the algae. As is typical off Bonaire, there are smaller fish and invertebrates such as banded coral shrimps and other cleaner shrimps, all of which are popular macro subjects.

The drop-off begins at 12m (40ft) and descends steeply to sand at 37m (120ft) with colourful purple vase sponges, orange elephant ear sponges and both green and purple tube sponges.

73 FOREST
★★★★

Location: Southeast of Southwest Corner (Site 72)
Access: By boat
Conditions: Medium to strong currents
Average Depth: 20m (65ft)
Maximum Depth: 40m (130ft)
Visibility: 30m (100ft)

Named after its forests of black coral, this is another of the best dive sites in the Caribbean. It is best dived in calm weather. Above the drop-off, the shallow water has elkhorn corals and prolific growth of gorgonian sea fans, sea rods and sea whips. The drop-off itself begins at 12m (40ft) and has large star corals and impressive gorgonians. The wall drops vertically to sand, covered in black coral, sponges and gorgonians, while below 15m (50ft), large orange elephant ear sponges are great for photography. Fish action is prolific, with big groupers, mahogany snappers, large horse-eye jacks, French and queen angelfish, black durgons, scrawled and whitespotted filefish, porcupine pufferfish, shoals of bluestriped grunts and innumerable small fish making this a memorable dive.

74 HANDS OFF
★★★★

Location: South coast of Klein Bonaire, east of Forest (Site 73)
Access: By boat
Conditions: Mild currents
Average Depth: 20m (65ft)
Maximum Depth: 40m (130ft)
Visibility: 30m (100ft)

Hands Off was originally established in 1981 as a site that was not to be dived by photographers, videographers, novice divers or those who were undergoing resort courses. The site was in effect a control for comparison with reefs where unlimited access was allowed. The intention was to assess the impact that inexperienced divers and camera-carrying divers were having on reefs.

The shallow water over the drop-off has elkhorn corals, gorgonian sea fans, sea rods and sea whips. The drop-off begins at 12m (40ft) and has large star corals and prolific gorgonian growth. The wall drops vertically to sand, covered in black coral, sponges and gorgonians, while below 15m (50ft) there are large orange elephant ear sponges. There are big groupers, mahogany and schoolmaster snappers, horse-eye jacks, French and queen angelfish, black durgons, scrawled and whitespotted filefish, porcupine pufferfish, peacock flounders and shoals of bluestriped grunts.

Above: *A yellowline arrow crab is camouflaged on a tube sponge.*

GETTING THERE

Bonaire's Flamingo International Airport is a five-minute drive south of Kralendijk. It has good air connections for such a small island.

By air from Europe, KLM has direct flights from Amsterdam, which has connections all over Europe. There are also many connections via Aruba, Curaçao and Caracas in Venezuela.

By air from the USA, ALM flies from Atlanta and Miami, and Air Aruba flies from Baltimore, Miami, Newark and Tampa. Air Jamaica also has a service.

Air Aruba and ALM connect with other Caribbean islands and South America.

Airport departure tax is US$10 for international flights and US$5.75 for flights within the Netherlands Antilles.

WHERE TO STAY

Bonaire's hotels are mostly along the leeward coast, many of them just north of Kralendijk. There are also villas for rent, both as separate entities or attached to hotels.

EXPENSIVE
Harbour Village Beach Resort
72 Kaya Gobernador Nicholaas Debrot; tel 599 7 7500, USA 800 424 0004; fax 599 7 7507; e-mail: harbourvil@aol.com
Bonaire's top luxury dive resort, originally targeted at the Dutch so it has a European atmosphere. The complex, as its name suggests, is like a small village complete with

a marina, 70 rooms and suites, several restaurants and most amenities.

The Plaza Resort Bonaire
80 Julio A. Abraham Boulevard, Kralendijk; tel 599 7 2500, USA 800 766 6016; fax 599 7 7133; e-mail: plaza@bonairenet.com
Voted by Americans as among the top ten dive resorts in the world. There are 224 suites and villas, each with a private patio or terrace. There are three restaurants, conference facilities and a casino.

MID-RANGE
Buddy Beach and Dive Resort
Kaya Gobernador Nicholaas Debrot, Kralendijk; tel 599 7 5080; fax 599 7 8647; e-mail: buddydive@ibm.net
Voted by American Divers as among the top fifteen dive resorts worldwide and by the German diving magazine *Tauchen* as the top dive resort in the Caribbean. Aimed mostly at the diver/snorkeller, it has four blocks with hotel rooms and one, two or three bedroom apartments, each with patios or balconies.

Captain Don's Habitat
P.O. Box 88, 103 Kaya Gobernador Nicholaas Debrot; tel 599 7 8290; fax 599 7 8240; e-mail: bonaire@habitatdiveresorts.com
Captain Don's Habitat was set up by and named after Don Stewart, the well-known pioneer of scuba diving in Bonaire. The resort is mainly sold as a diving package – your room key is on a band that can be

worn on a wrist in the water – and everyone is very friendly. Popular with American and British divers. Unashamedly aimed at divers, there are 93 rooms, apartments and villas for up to 6 persons.

Divi Flamingo Beach Resort & Casino
40 Julio A. Abraham Boulevard; tel 599 7 8285; fax 599 7 8238; e-mail: charlesp@diviresorts.com
Bonaire's first hotel and dive facility, originally managed by Captain Don Stewart. The 145 rooms and studio rooms are being renovated and the resort boasts that it has the 'worlds first barefoot casino'; ie. it allows casual dress!

Lac Bay Resort
PO Box 261, 64 Kamindo Sorobon; tel 599 7 8198; fax 599 7 5686; e-mail: lacbay@bonairelive.com
In a protected nature area, Lac Bay and the jointly owned Sorobon (naturist) Beach resort are the only two resorts located on the windward coast. The bay is ideal for windsurfing. There are 11 units ranging from one-bedroom condominiums to villas and studios.

Lions Dive Hotel Bonaire
91 Kaya Gobernador Nicholaas Debrot; tel 599 7 5580; fax 599 7 5680; e-mail:

lionsdive@bonairenet.com
This was formerly the Coral Regency Resort.
There are 31 one or two bedroom suites.

Sand Dollar Condominium Resort
PO Box 262, 79 Kaya Gobernador Nicholaas
Debrot; tel 599 7 8738, USA 800 288 4773;
fax 599 7 8760; e-mail:
sanddollar@bonairenet.com
Voted by Americans as the second best
resort worldwide. There are 85 one to three
bedroom condominiums; the resort runs a
popular Ocean Classroom for children.

INEXPENSIVE
Avanti Bungalows
9 Punt Vierkant; tel 599 7 8405; fax 599 7
8605; e-mail: hhh@bonairelive.com
Four bungalows of one or two-bedrooms,
each with a kitchenette.

Bruce Bowker's Carib Inn
PO Box 68, 46 Julio A. Abraham Boulevard;
tel 599 7 8819; fax 599 7 5295; e-mail:
bruce@caribinn.com
Bruce Bowker was one of Captain Don's
early students. Voted by American divers as
the top value-for-money dive operator and
resort, it prides itself on allowing you to
relax without outside communications
distracting you. It is small and intimate, but
with a very well equipped dive centre. There
are ten, one or two-bedroom apartments
and villas.

Leeward Inn
60 Kaya Grandi, Kralendijk; tel 599 7 5516;
fax 599 7 5517
A cheap guest house but in town so you
have to allow for the extra cost of transport.
The popular and cosy café and bar are a
favourite meeting place for both tourists and
locals and it is locally famous for its home-
made pizzas.

The Great Escape
97 E.E.G. Boulevard; tel 599 7 7488;
fax 599 7 7488
There are ten apartments and again
relatively cheap, but you must allow for the
additional cost of transport.

WHERE TO EAT

Bonaire has some of the top restaurants in
the Caribbean. Many hotels and resorts have
restaurants good enough to attract non-
resident clientele and there are others to suit
all tastes.

CHINESE CUISINE
China Garden
47 Kaya Grandi; tel 599 7 8480
Chinese food.

INTERNATIONAL CUISINE
Beefeater
12 Kaya Grandi, Kralendijk; tel 599 7 7776
Moderate prices and also serves
vegetarian food.

De Tuin Eetcafé
9 Kaya L. D. Gerharts, Kralendijk;
tel 599 7 2999
Garden dining in a restored Bonairean home
and a cyber restaurant.

Green Parrot
Sand Dollar Condominium Resort, 79
Kaya Gobernador Nicholaas Debrot;
tel 599 7 5454
Popular with guests at the Sand Dollar
Condominium Resort. It is on the
waterfront, so you can watch the fish eat
scraps thrown in by the waiters.
International menu including half-pound US
beef 'Parrot Burgers'.

Mona Lisa
15 Kaya Grandi, Kralendijk; tel 599 7 8718;
fax 599 7 5498
Dutch and French cuisine served in portions
large enough to satisfy the hungriest divers;
reservations recommended.

Richards Waterfront Dining
60 Julio A. Abraham Boulevard, Kralendijk;
tel 599 7 5263
Popular with visitors.

Rum Runners
Captain Don's Habitat, 103 Kaya
Gobernador Nicholaas Debrot;
tel 599 7 7303
A waterfront restaurant popular with guests
staying at Captain Don's Habitat.
International menu, friendly service and
many themed nights where different cuisine
is served.

'T Ankertje
17 Kaya C. E. B. Hellmund, Kralendijk;
tel 599 7 5216; fax 599 7 2943
Known as the 'local' restaurant, small and
cheap with no frills.

ITALIAN CUISINE
Croccantino
48 Kaya Grandi, Kralendijk; tel 599 7 5025
A restored historic town house with
Italian cuisine. It is possible to eat out in
the garden.

MEXICAN CUISINE
Captain Wook's
Harbour Village Marina, Kaya Gobernador
Nicholaas Debrot; tel 599 7 7500;
fax 599 7 7507

Casual dining on Mexican specialities beside
the marina at Harbour Village. Not open
for breakfast.

SPANISH CUISINE
Admirals Tavern
Harbour Village Marina, Kaya
Gobernador Nicholaas Debrot; tel 599 7
7500; fax 599 7 7507
At the bottom of the lighthouse at
Harbour Village Marina. It specializes in
local and Spanish seafood. Not open
for breakfast.

DIVE FACILITIES

Apart from Captain Don's Habitat, all
other dive operators on Bonaire are
concessionary operators attached to hotels.
Most resorts have dive operators on their
premises, and you can usually pre-book
dive packages together with your
accommodation for better deals. The larger
dive operators have equipment for sale as
well as hire.

Black Durgon Scuba Center
Black Durgon Inn, PO Box 200;
tel 599 7 5736, USA 800 526 2370;
fax 599 7 8846; e-mail:
bkdurgon@bonairelive.com
Instruction up to Open Water Diver level
offered in Dutch, English, German
and Spanish.

Blue Divers
2 Kaya Den Tere, Kralendijk;
tel 599 7 6860; fax 599 7 6865; e-mail:
bluedivers@bonairenet.com
Specialize in small groups. Instruction up to
Assistant Instructor level offered in Dutch,
English and German.

Bon Bini Divers Bonaire, N.V.
Lions Dive Resort (formally Coral
Regency Resort), 90 Kaya Gobernador
Nicholaas Debrot; tel 599 7 5425;
fax 599 7 4425; e-mail:
bonbinidiv@aol.com
Instruction up to Assistant Instructor level
offered in Dutch, English and German.

Bruce Bowker's Carib Inn
PO Box 68, 46 Julio A. Abraham Boulevard;
tel 599 7 8819; fax 599 7 5295; e-mail:
bruce@caribinn.com
Voted by American divers as the best
value resort in the world, it is proud to
be small and has a very well equipped
dive centre.

Buddy Dive
Buddy Beach & Dive Resort, Kaya
Gobernador Nicholaas Debrot, Kralendijk;

Netherlands. The economic boom that followed brought about modernization, including a moveable pontoon bridge to link the two main districts of Willemstad, separated by one of the largest natural harbours in the western hemisphere.

The boom years collapsed when automation cut the refinery workforce from 18,500 to 4,000. Shell sold the refinery to the Netherlands Antilles Government in 1985 and they in turn leased it to an affiliate of Petroleos de Venezuela S.A. Nowadays, offshore banking is an important income though tourism forms Curaçao's second largest industry.

> ### MANSALIÑA TREES
>
> Also called manchineel, mansaliña trees provide shade on many of Curaçao's beaches and in the grounds of some hotels. Their small round yellow or green fruit is extremely poisonous. The sap of the tree can also irritate the skin and can cause a severe allergic reaction. If you experience a mild reaction, bathe the area with cold water. If you suffer a severe reaction, you will require antihistamine cream and possibly antihistamine tablets.

LOCAL HIGHLIGHTS

Willemstad, the island's capital, lies on the southern coast at Santa Anna Bay. It was formerly a fortified town of strategic importance and is noted for its Dutch colonial architecture in bright colours. Relatively small but usually very busy, walking is probably the best way to see the town.

The Queen Emma Pontoon Bridge is the largest floating pedestrian bridge in the world. The 'Lady', as it is known to the local inhabitants, was originally built in 1888 by the American Consul Leonard Burlington Smith. At 213m (700ft) long, it was regarded as a feat of engineering in its day, and a toll was charged to cross the bridge though people who were too poor to afford shoes were entitled to cross it for free; the present construction, the third,

Opposite: *The historical archives building in Willemstad used to be a merchant's house.*
Below: *The present-day Queen Emma Pontoon Bridge was constructed in 1939.*

CHRISTOFFEL NATIONAL PARK

The volcanic crest of Curaçao's highest point, Mount Christoffel, is in the northwest corner of the island. Here 1821ha (4500 acres) of wilderness surrounding the mountain have been gazetted as a natural reserve. The park contains a wide variety of animals and plants; over 100 shy, Curaçao white-tailed deer can be found along with wild goats and blue iguanas, and some rare orchids.

At the park entrance the old Savonet plantation house is now a nature conservancy, visitors' centre and a Museum of Natural and Cultural History. A guidebook covers the park's botanical, geological, and zoological features and three marked trails: the Zorgvlied Trail runs along the northern side of the island, passing the Indian caves; the Zevenbergen Trail covers the southwest corner of the park, featuring spectacular views and two rare species of orchid; and the Christoffel Trail has great vistas and opportunities for bird-watching.

The park is open Monday to Saturday from 08:00 to 16:00 and from 06:00 to 15:00 on Sunday; admission is US$9. Guided tours are available by jeep or on foot and each day guides escort groups of up to eight people to an observation tower to watch the deer for ten-minutes between 16:00 and 18:30.

Opposite: *Various arched limestone bridges exist along the windward side of Curaçao.*

was built in 1939. The bridge links the two shopping districts of Punda and Otrobanda, swinging open as often as thirty times a day to let ships pass into or out of the bay – the pontoons can also be seen to move constantly on the waves. Beside the Queen Emma Bridge is the Floating Market, where boats arrive from Venezuela to set up market selling fresh fish, vegetables, fruits, and spices.

The imposing Queen Juliana Bridge is for motorized traffic only and has four traffic lanes. Rising 56m (185ft) above the bay and spanning 488m (1600ft), it took 14 years and cost 15 lives to complete.

Many 17th- and 18th-century fortresses ring the harbour; originally built as defence from pirates as well as the English and French navies. At the centre of historic Willemstad, stands the mustard-coloured Fort Amsterdam, dating from 1769. The fort's church doubled as a store for provisions in case of siege and a cannonball is still embedded in the church's southwest wall; nearby is the present Governor's Residence.

Nearby Fort Waterfort (Waterfort Arches), just outside Punda, was originally constructed in 1634 and rebuilt in 1827. During World War II, Allied Forces and anti-aircraft guns were accommodated here. Opposite the harbour entrance from Fort Waterfort, Fort Riffort is an impressive structure built in 1828. In World War II a steel net was stretched across the bay between the two against enemy shipping. Once housing government departments, the ramparts have been restored and now there are two restaurants here. Fort Waakzaamheid was beseiged for 26 days by Captain Bligh of 'Mutiny On the Bounty' fame in 1804. An English cannonball is imbedded in one of its walls. Fort Nassau (Fort Orange Nassau) was built in 1797 and has been preserved in much of its original state – except for the addition of a discotheque.

Also in Willemstad, the Mikve Israel-Emanuel is the oldest synagogue in continuous use in the Americas, founded in 1732 by Sephardic Jews escaping oppression in Portugal and Spain. The floor is carpeted in sand, as in the days of the Inquisition when the Jews prayed on sand to avoid being heard. The Beth Haim cemetery goes back as far as the 17th century, and many religious articles from the original Jewish community are on display at the Jewish Historical & Cultural Museum in the synagogue compound.

The Scharloo district has imposing old wealthy merchant's houses. At 77 Scharlooweg the Central Historical Archives are kept in a mansion painted green and called 'Bolo di Bruid', Papamiento for 'Bride's Cake', by the local inhabitants. The Bolívar Museum is an eight-sided Octagon House that provided sanctuary for the sisters of Simón Bolívar when they were in exile. Other attractions include the Sea Aquarium and even an ostrich farm. Near to the airport the Hato Caves, covering 4900 sq m (5860 sq yd), include fascinating stalactite and stalagmite limestone formations, a waterfall and a colony of long-nose bats. A wooded trail leads to Caiquetio Indian frescoes.

Above: *Lavender stovepipe sponges inhabit deeper reefs and walls.*

7 PLAYA JEREMI

★★★★★★★★

Location: Northwest coast, off Playa Jeremi, near Landhuis Jeremi
Access: By boat or shore
Conditions: Normally calm
Average Depth: 18m (60ft)
Maximum Depth: 40m+ (130ft+)
Visibility: 30m (100ft)

Playa Jeremi is a pretty cove with a smooth beach that is protected from most of the weather. It is good for shore diving and night diving. The site is known for its flying gurnards, found on the seabed in 5m (16ft) of water.

The sandy bottom features urchins, conchs, lizardfish, goatfish and peacock flounders. To reach the coral, swim over the sand west to the mouth of the cove. The centre of the cove is deeper than its edge; the corals begin at 9–12m (30–40ft) near the edges of the cove and between 12–15m (40–50ft) in the centre. The further out you swim, the better the coral. By the north wall of the cove is a large rock sticking out of the water – the wall and this rock are covered with orange *Tubastrea* cup corals. Large trumpetfish group nearby and there are copper and glassy sweepers (*Pempheris schomburgki*) beneath the ledges.

8 PLAYA LAGUN (LAGOEN)

★★★★★★★★

Location: Northwest coast, off Playa Lagun, at the southern end of the village of Lagun
Access: By boat or shore
Conditions: Normally calm
Average Depth: 18m (60ft)
Maximum Depth: 40m+ (130ft+)
Visibility: 30m (100ft)

One of the island's top dives, Playa Lagun is a small cove enclosed by cliffs. This site is very easy to shore dive as you can almost drive up to the water. The best entry from the shore is to the southeast, where there are several small caves. To see the site's features, swim out to the drop-off at 10m (30ft). Be aware that the drop-off then drops at 45° to a second drop-off at 45m (150ft), which is beyond sport diving depths.

The first drop-off features good stony coral, gorgonian and sponge coverage, with the sponges attracting hawksbill turtles. The fish life here is profuse, including lizardfish, rainbow runners, rock beauties, blackbar soldierfish, bluespotted cornetfish and parrotfish.

9 SANTU PRETU

★★★★★★★★★

Location: Northwest coast, off San Nicolas, just south of the inlet at Santa Cruz
Access: By boat or shore
Conditions: Normally calm
Average Depth: 18m (60ft)
Maximum Depth: 40m+ (130ft+)
Visibility: 30m (100ft)

Boca Santa Pretu is Papiamento for 'Black Sand Beach', referring to the vein of black volcanic sand found here, which illustrates the volcanic origin of the island. If shore diving, enter the water at the northwest of the beach and swim towards the centre of the cove, past the garden eels, to the drop-off at 9–12m (30–40ft). Here you will find good stony corals and extravagant gorgonian growth, sponges and rich fish life, including parrotfish, rock beauties, cero (*Scomberomorus regalis*), banded and foureye butterflyfish, blackbar soldierfish, trumpetfish and bluespotted cornetfish. The sponges also attract hawksbill turtles.

10 MUSHROOM FOREST & THE CAVE

★★★★

Location: Northwest coast, southwest of Santa Cruz, the point south of Santu Pretu, north of Sponge Forest (Site 11)
Access: By boat
Conditions: There can be a strong current.
Average Depth: 13m (43ft)
Maximum Depth: 40m+ (130ft+)
Visibility: 30m (100ft)

One of Curaçao's top dives, Mushroom Forest was so named because of the many large coral heads of mountainous star coral that have been eroded at their base to resemble mushrooms. American divers vote this site as the best in Curaçao – but do compare it with Watamula (Site 1) if you can. The sea floor is complex and the coral heads look similar and disorientating, so take your compass or a local dive guide. Although there

is a drop-off, the main area of interest is on the relatively flat, inshore shelf at 12–15m (40–50ft).

This is a diverse site, so take time to have a good look in as many cracks and crannies as you can. The 3m (10ft) coral heads are a riot of colour: anemones, flower and brain corals, lobsters, drums, moray eels, conchs, trunkfish, porcupine pufferfish, rock beauties, parrotfish, snappers, peacock flounders, trumpetfish, bluespotted cornetfish (*Fistularia tabacaria*), redspotted hawkfish (*Amblycirrhitus pinos*), Creole wrasse and turtles are just a few of the animals to be found. Sleeping nurse sharks are also regularly seen here.

There is a dive buoy that guides you to the sites. Mushroom Forest is a little beyond the buoy, while The Cave is directly inshore from it, in the cliffs at the water's edge. The Cave is only 6m (20ft) deep and with a huge entrance, so you do not need to be cave-certified to enjoy the cavern. Shoals of sweepers dash around, orange *Tubastrea* cup corals encrust the roof, while slipper lobsters crawl around the walls and lizardfish and scorpionfish hide on the bottom. Remember to bring a dive light.

11 SPONGE FOREST

★★★★★★★★★

Location: West coast, off San Nicolas, northwest of Playa Hulu (Site 12)
Access: By boat
Conditions: Usually fairly calm with little current
Average Depth: 20m (65ft)
Maximum Depth: 40m+ (130ft+)
Visibility: 30m (100ft)

Protected by a point of land to the southeast of Boca Hulu, the sandy shelf by the shore here has little of interest other than small brain corals. However the slope, which begins at about 12m (40ft) and drops gradually to sand at 40m (130ft), features stony corals and gorgonians and very large basket and branched sponges in the deeper areas. There is rich fish life including damselfish, sergeant majors, chromis, rock beauties, pufferfish, trumpetfish, bluespotted cornetfish and French and queen angelfish.

12 PLAYA HULU

★★★★★★

Location: West coast, off San Nicolas
Access: By boat or shore
Conditions: Usually fairly calm with little current
Average Depth: 20m (65ft)
Maximum Depth: 40m+ (130ft+)
Visibility: 30m (100ft)

If shore diving, enter the water on the southeast side of the beach and swim out to a coral-covered slope descending from 9–40m (30–130ft). The shallow waters attract Christmas tree worms and abundant fish life, while deeper down there are black corals and featherduster worms.

13 REDIHO
★★★★

Location: West coast, off San Nicolas, south of Pos Spano
Access: By boat or shore
Conditions: Choppy with strong currents
Average Depth: 20m (65ft)
Maximum Depth: 40m+ (130ft+)
Visibility: 30m (100ft)

Rediho is exposed to the open sea, so conditions are often rough, though the nutrient-rich currents produce healthy marine life. The dive and the reef profile are similar to that of the nearby Black Coral Garden (site 14). A steep drop-off begins at 12m (40ft) and descends below sport diving depths. There are most local Caribbean species here, including butterflyfish, trumpetfish, trunkfish, chromis, sergeant majors, frogfish, seahorses, moray eels, shoals of grunts, snappers, Creole wrasse and jacks. Turtles are common.

14 BLACK CORAL GARDEN
★★★★

Location: West coast, off San Nicolas, south of Pos Spano
Access: By boat or shore
Conditions: Choppy with strong currents
Average Depth: 20m (65ft)
Maximum Depth: 40m+ (130ft+)
Visibility: 30m (100ft)

There is no shelter from the open sea here, so conditions can be rough. The steep drop-off begins at 12m (40ft) and descends below sport diving depths. In deeper water the drop-off supports a colossal black coral forest. There is almost every Caribbean species present, including chromis, damselfish, sergeant majors, frogfish, seahorses, moray eels, shoals of grunts, snappers, Creole wrasse and jacks, lone barracuda, manta rays and whale sharks. Turtles are also common visitors to the area.

Below: *Spanish hogfish constantly swim about and show little fear of divers.*

Above: *A diver takes a close-up photograph of a sponge, taking care not to touch the subject.*
Below: *Hawksbill turtles are common in areas with lots of sponges.*

15 HELL'S CORNER
★★★★

Location: West coast, off the south part of San Nicolas, the corner of the reef out west from Santa Martha Bay
Access: By boat
Conditions: Sometimes calm, but usually rough with strong currents
Average Depth: 20m (65ft)
Maximum Depth: 40m+ (130ft+)
Visibility: 30m (100ft)
This site has no mooring so it is treated as a drift dive. As there is no shelter from the open sea, it is for advanced divers only. The current usually runs east to west parallel to the shore, but it can have large eddies and down-currents. If you get into trouble there is a sandy beach just to the north that is used as an emergency exit. A shallow shelf with some staghorn coral reaches the drop-off at 9m (30ft) and then falls off gradually at about 45° to sand at 40m (130ft). Large brain, pillar and star corals, gorgonians and turtles are found on the upper part of the slope and large pelagic fish as well as reef fish are often seen.

16 MAKO'S MOUNTAIN
★★★★

Location: West coast, off the south end of San Nicolas, at the point of land jutting out to sea west of the entrance to Santa Martha Bay
Access: By boat
Conditions: Choppy seas and strong currents; snorkelling is only possible on very calm days
Average Depth: 20m (65ft)
Maximum Depth: 40m+ (130ft+)
Visibility: 30m (100ft)
Similar conditions to Hells Corner (Site 15) mean that this site is only for experienced divers. The mooring buoy is in 5m (16ft) and the steep slope of the drop-off descends into the depths. The currents produce healthy marine life including sponges, gorgonian sea rods, sea plumes, sea fans and sea whips, together with most Caribbean reef fish and many pelagic species.

17 AIRPLANE WRECK
★★★★★★★★

Location: West coast, off Coral Cliff Beach
Access: By boat or shore; from the shore, enter between the two breakwaters protecting the calm lagoon
Conditions: Sheltered, usually some current and swell
Average Depth: 15m (50ft)
Maximum Depth: 40m+ (130ft+)
Visibility: 30m (100ft)

Airplane Wreck is one of several dive sites that can be reached from Coral Cliff Beach, where there are good facilities. Straight out from the breakwater, a buoy marks the remains of a Cessna aeroplane at 9m (30ft). The shallows are sand and rock rubble, but the reef descends gently into deep water where there are lots of corals, sponges and reef fish, including angelfish, peacock flounders, Creole wrasse, rock beauties, banded and foureye butterflyfish, scrawled filefish, moray eels and yellowtail snappers. This is a good site for a night dive.

18 HARRY'S HOLE/WET SUIT CITY/ CORAL CLIFF DROP-OFF
★★★★★★

Location: West coast, off Coral Cliff Beach
Access: By boat or shore
Conditions: Some chop and surge – dive only in calm conditions
Average Depth: 6m (20ft)
Maximum Depth: 40m+ (130ft+)
Visibility: 30m (100ft)
This site was previously called Wet Suit City because of the need for protection against fire coral and large bristle (fire) worms (*Hermodice carunculata*) in the surge. Enter the water at a sandy spot just to the left of the left-hand breakwater and swim out southeast to 3m (10ft) deep, turning left parallel to the shore. This is an interesting area where stands of fire coral harbour juvenile brown chromis; garden eels and scorpionfish can be found on the sand.

The drop-off used to be called Coral Cliff Drop-Off, because of the site's proximity to Coral Cliff. It begins at 12m (40ft) and slopes gently to a series of shelves at about 18m (60ft), then slopes more steeply to below 20m (100ft). There is light coral cover with large sandy

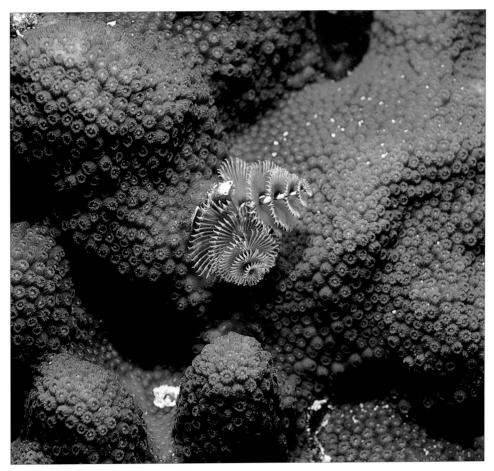

Above: *Christmas tree worms burrow into coral, leaving two fan-shaped spiral whorls protruding.*
Opposite: *A boulder star coral grows above a leathery barrel sponge.*

areas between the coral heads; some of the shelves and the area at the base of the drop-off attract garden eel colonies. In deeper water there are gorgonian sea fans and vase and basket sponges.

19 PLAYA HUNDU LOST ANCHOR
★★★

Location: West coast, south of Santa Martha Bay
Access: By boat or shore
Conditions: Can have challenging conditions, with choppy wave action and current
Average Depth: 20m (65ft)
Maximum Depth: 40m+ (130ft+)
Visibility: 30m (100ft)
Playa Hundu means 'Deep Beach' in Papiamento. The drop-off begins at 9m (30ft) and descends steeply past a

large anchor at 23m (75ft) down to sand at 40m (130ft). Most Caribbean reef fish can be found as well as gorgonians and corals.

20 BOCA GRANDI
★★★★★★

Location: West coast, just north of San Juan Bay
Access: By boat or shore
Conditions: Usually fairly calm with little current
Average Depth: 20m (65ft)
Maximum Depth: 40m+ (130ft+)
Visibility: 30m (100ft)
A compass is useful to access this site, as the drop-off is quite a long swim out northwest and very gradual. The coral cover increases with depth and at Inner San Juan Bay there are large star coral heads at 15m (50ft).

The bottom is relatively flat and slopes gently into deeper water. Eels, spotted drums and lobsters inhabit many of the nooks and crannies beneath the coral heads.

21 PLAYA MANSALIÑA
★★★★★★

Location: West coast, just south of San Juan Bay
Access: By boat or shore
Conditions: Usually fairly calm with little current
Average Depth: 20m (65ft)
Maximum Depth: 40m+ (130ft+)
Visibility: 30m (100ft)
The diving here is similar to that at Boca Grandi (Site 20). The coral cover increases with depth and there are large star coral heads at 15m (50ft). The bottom shelves gently into deeper water. Eels, spotted drums (*Equetus punctatus*) and lobsters may be found in many of the nooks and crannies beneath the coral heads. Be aware that the nearby beach, Playa Mansaliña, is shaded with Mansaliña (Manchineel) trees that have poisonous fruit and sap that can cause skin irritations.

The fish life here includes French and queen angelfish, peacock flounders, Creole wrasse, rock beauties, banded and foureye butterflyfish, scrawled filefish, moray eels, pufferfish, scorpionfish, trumpetfish, grunts and yellowtail snappers.

22 BIG SPONGE/MIKE'S REEF
★★★★★★★★

Location: West coast, north of Playa Largu (Site 23)
Access: By boat
Conditions: Choppy with some current
Average Depth: 20m (65ft)
Maximum Depth: 40m+ (130ft+)
Visibility: 30m (100ft)
...was originally named Mike's Reef after Mike ... Dive Operations Manager at Habitat ... as instrumental in putting this site on ... is so-called because it used to have ... and as a photographer's dream. ... lobster...ng into the sponge were French a... and fourey...) of water and the and pufferfish. ...re shelving off ...brain, black ... whips, ...ludes

23 PLAYA LARGU
★★★★★★★

Location: West coast, off Playa Largu
Access: By boat or shore
Conditions: Usually fairly calm with little current
Average Depth: 20m (65ft)
Maximum Depth: 40m+ (130ft+)
Visibility: 30m (100ft)
This site has brain and star corals, gorgonian sea rods and sea whips. The reef fish life includes French and queen angelfish, rock beauties, banded and foureye butterflyfish, trumpetfish, parrotfish, filefish, goatfish and pufferfish.

24 LOWER HOUSE/CAS ABAO
★★★★★★★

Location: West coast, off Cas Abao Beach
Access: By boat or shore
Conditions: Usually fairly calm with little current
Average Depth: 20m (65ft)
Maximum Depth: 40m+ (130ft+)
Visibility: 30m (100ft)
This site features a shallow shelf near to the shore with a drop-off at about 9m (30ft), which falls off sharply to

sand below 40m (130ft). The slope is very rich in marine life, especially in crevices beneath the coral heads; you can see lobsters and often several spotted drums together under one coral head. Towards the deeper part of the slope, large orange elephant ear sponges are found.

25 THE VALLEY/PORT MARIE
★★★★★★★★★

Location: West coast, off Port Marie Beach, south of Cas Abao
Access: By boat or shore
Conditions: Usually fairly calm with little current
Average Depth: 18m (60ft)
Maximum Depth: 40m+ (130ft+)
Visibility: 30m (100ft)
Also called Port Marie, The Valley is one of the island's top sites. Two healthy parallel reefs with a 'valley' in between are home to a wide variety of reef life. Often there are fish here that are rare at other sites, including small nurse sharks.

The mooring buoy in the centre of the bay is at 9m (30ft). Swimming straight out will take you over the first reef at 15m (50ft), then crossing the sandy valley leads to the second reef at about 18m (60ft). The Valley has profuse fish life including angelfish, parrotfish, groupers, brown chromis, yellowtail snapper, triggerfish, trumpetfish, bluespotted cornetfish, turtles, lobsters and stingrays. It is a good site for night diving.

26 DAAIBOOI
★★★★★★

Location: West coast, south of Port Marie beach
Access: By boat or shore
Conditions: Usually fairly calm with little current
Average Depth: 20m (65ft)
Maximum Depth: 40m+ (130ft+)
Visibility: 30m (100ft)
The swim out to the site is sheltered by high cliffs and there is no current until you reach the mouth of the bay. The shallow water has elkhorn corals and the moderate slope has brain, pillar and star corals, gorgonians and abundant reef fish. This is a pretty dive.

27 SAINT MARIE/RIF
★★★★★★★★★

Location: West coast, off Habitat Curaçao
Access: By boat or shore
Conditions: Usually fairly calm with some current
Average Depth: 20m (65ft)
Maximum Depth: 40m+ (130ft+)
Visibility: 30m (100ft)

This site is Habitat Curaçao's House Reef, the best house reef on the island. As with their operation on Bonaire, Habitat Curaçao have two jetties, one for boats and one for shore diving. A yellow rope along the seabed extends the few metres out to the drop-off and then down it. It is thus easy for divers to find and make their way to and from the shore diving jetty without getting near to any boats using the boat jetty.

The shallow water features elkhorn coral, palometa (*Trachinotus goodei*), spotted moray eels swimming free, parrotfish, rock beauties, peacock flounders, lizardfish, banded and foureye butterflyfish, while over the drop-off there are also French angelfish, porcupine pufferfish, trunkfish, bluespotted cornetfish, trumpetfish, sergeant majors, grunts, snappers and shoals of goatfish. The drop-off begins at 5m (16ft) and as you get deeper the stony corals, sponges and gorgonians become denser, sheltering a multitude of invertebrates including lobsters, banded coral shrimps and Christmas tree worms.

28 LIGHT TOWER
★★★★

Location: Southwest coast, west of Cape St Marie
Access: By boat
Conditions: Rough with challenging currents
Average Depth: 20m (65ft)
Maximum Depth: 40m+ (130ft+)
Visibility: 30m (100ft)
Named after the light tower on the cape, this is a drift dive for advanced divers only. The drop-off is at 7m (23ft) from where a steep slope descends into deep water. The strong currents produce large and healthy marine life including a shoal of barracuda. Hammerhead sharks have been seen here.

29 SELDOM
★★★★

Location: Southwest coast, east of Cape St Marie
Access: By boat
Conditions: Rough seas and challenging currents
Average Depth: 20m (65ft)
Maximum Depth: 40m+ (130ft+)
Visibility: 30m (100ft)
'Seldom' dived because of the difficult cond[...] site is for advanced divers only. The drop[...] 7m (23ft) and descends into deep water[...] about as steep as you get in Cura[...] spectacular with many barracuda[...] horse-eye jacks as well as reef f[...]

Opposite: *A pair o[...]
together across[...]*

water from the police jetty. The drop-off begins at about 9–12m (30–40ft) and slopes down into deep water at about 45°. There are star corals, gorgonian sea plumes, sea rods and sea whips, while the fish life includes moray eels, parrotfish, rock beauties, peacock flounders, lizardfish, banded and foureye butterflyfish, angelfish, pufferfish, trunkfish, trumpetfish, damselfish, chromis, grunts, snappers and shoals of goatfish.

32 CAR WRECKS
★★★★★★

Location: Southwest coast, just south of Vaersen Bay
Access: By boat or shore
Conditions: Normally calm
Average Depth: 20m (65ft)
Maximum Depth: 40m+ (130ft+)
Visibility: 30m (100ft)
This is where many old cars (and the barge that transported them) lie along the drop-off at 28m (92ft). Descending into deep water, the drop-off has profuse marine life. There are brain corals, gorgonian sea plumes, sea rods and sea whips and the fish life includes moray eels, parrotfish, rock beauties, peacock flounders, lizardfish, foureye butterflyfish, French angelfish, porcupine pufferfish, trunkfish, trumpetfish, damselfish, chromis, surgeonfish, grunts and snappers.

SEA-GRASS

Sea-grasses are the pastures of the ocean. They are found in estuaries or shallow coastal waters with mud or sand bottoms, where they stabilize the substrate, provide food and shelter and act as a breeding ground and nursery for many marine creatures.

Sea-grasses are neither true grasses nor seaweed (algae); they are in fact flowering plants with roots, stems, leaves and flowers. Their underground stems (rhizomes) and roots anchor the plants to the soft bottom and, as with land plants, the roots take up nutrients. Since the substrate where they grow is poor in oxygen it is the leaves that take up oxygen, which is transported along canals to their rhizomes and roots.

The leaves of sea-grasses also absorb sunlight for photosynthesis, so that water, carbon dioxide and other chemicals can be converted into nutrients and oxygen. One square metre (1.196 sq yd) of sea-grass produces an average of ten litres (17.6 pints) of oxygen each day and research has deduced that 100 sq m (120 sq yd) can support 500 tonnes (492 tons) of fish a year.

As with flowering land plants, sea-grasses produce pollen, which drifts with the currents, attaches itself to other flowers and fertilizes them to produce seed. Sea-grass beds mainly grow out horizontally, due to the horizontal stems that continually creep outwards along the sand.

Dugongs, green turtles, some herbivorous fish and many invertebrates feed on sea-grasses. They also slow down fast-flowing water and provide refuge for many immature fish, crabs, lobsters and prawns.

---

33 HALFWAY
★★★★★★

Location: Southwest coast, halfway between Vaersen Bay and Boca St Michiel
Access: By boat
Conditions: Normally calm
Average Depth: 20m (65ft)
Maximum Depth: 40m+ (130ft+)
Visibility: 30m (100ft)
Swim over the sandy plateau with its stingrays and garden eels to the drop-off at 9m (30ft). The drop-off descends into deep water with excellent corals, gorgonians and reef fish. There are brain and star corals, gorgonian sea plumes, sea rods and sea whips and the fish life includes spotted moray eels, parrotfish, peacock flounders, lizardfish, foureye butterflyfish, French angelfish, porcupine pufferfish, trunkfish, trumpetfish, soldierfish, sergeant majors, groupers, grunts and snappers. Frogfish and seahorses are occasional visitors.

34 BOCA SAMI
★★★★★★

Location: Southwest coast, off Boca St Michiel, west of Boca Sami, in front of The Wederfoort Dive Center
Access: By boat or shore
Conditions: Normally calm
Average Depth: 20m (65ft)
Maximum Depth: 40m+ (130ft+)
Visibility: 30m (100ft)
The drop-off descends from 12m (40ft) into deep water, with excellent marine life including turtles and dolphins. There are brain, star and pencil corals, gorgonian sea plumes, sea rods and sea whips, moray eels, parrotfish, peacock flounders, lizardfish, foureye butterflyfish, French and queen angelfish, porcupine pufferfish, trunkfish, trumpetfish, grunts, surgeonfish, fusiliers and snappers.

35 SNAKE BAY
★★★★★★

Location: Southwest coast, off Boca St Michiel, southwest of Boca Sami
Access: By boat or shore
Conditions: Normally calm
Average Depth: 20m (65ft)
Maximum Depth: 40m+ (130ft+)
Visibility: 30m (100ft)
The name refers to the moray eels seen here – the drop-off itself is the same as that of Boca Sami (Site 34). The drop-off starts at 12m (40ft) and descends into deep water. You will find brain and star corals, gorgonian sea

Established in 1983, the Curaçao Underwater Park stretches from Princess Beach Hotel to the eastern tip of the island, and includes some of Curaçao's finest reefs. Running from the high-water mark to the 60m (200ft) depth contour, the park covers a total surface area of 600ha (1483 acres) of reef and 436ha (1077 acres) of inner bays.

Past research by CARMABI indicated that coastal development, pollution, spear fishing and poaching were causing serious degeneration to the reef, fish populations were falling and black coral was becoming rare. The marine park was therefore set up with the main objective of protecting the reef and fish populations while at the same time stimulating recreational tourism activities in a sustainable manner. STINAPA obtained a grant from the World Wide Fund For Nature (WWF) to develop the Curaçao Underwater Park and is responsible for its day-to-day management.

Mooring Buoys

Each dive site has a public mooring buoy specifically for use by visitors to the park. The buoys are anchored with a concrete block of at least one ton. The design of the mooring does not include a chain, so as to prevent a barren area developing around the mooring due to a swaying anchor chain. This means that the strength of the mooring depends entirely on the weight of the block and the length of rope paid out by the boat that ties up to it. The boat's skipper must pay out a length of at least $1^1/_2$ times the length of the boat in order to be safely moored. If properly used the mooring buoys are highly dependable and can safely secure boats of up to 12m (36ft) in length under normal weather conditions.

Park Rules

Do not take any plants or animals, dead or alive, from the reefs other than by hook and line fishing. Collecting coral is a criminal offence.

Do not sit or step on corals, they are living animals!

Avoid any unintentional contact with corals by good buoyancy control.

Do not anchor in the coral, use the mooring buoys or select a sandy area.

Do not spear fish.

Help to keep the park clean.

Below: *A brown chromis lays its eggs in the Curaçao Underwater Park.*

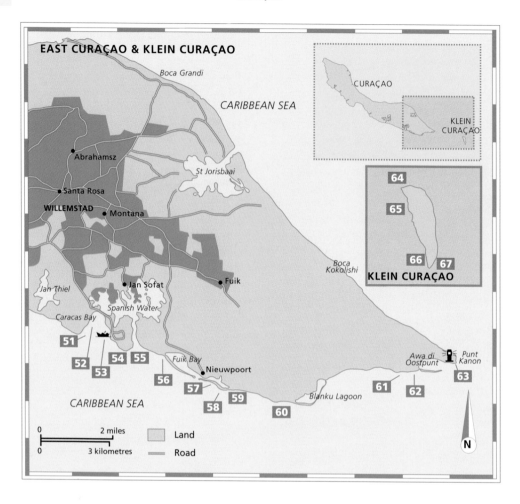

East Curaçao and Klein Curaçao

51 KABES DI BARANKA/BEACON POINT
★★★★★★★

Location: South coast, near the entrance to Caracas Bay
Access: By boat
Conditions: Choppy with strong current
Average Depth: 20m (65ft)
Maximum Depth: 40m+ (130ft+)
Visibility: 30m (100ft)
Also called Beacon Point, Kabes di Baranka means 'head of the rock' in Papiamento. Near the mooring buoy there is a large pillar coral in the shallows, while from the drop-off at 6m (20ft) a wall descends to a ledge at 33m (110ft) before shelving into deeper water. There are healthy corals, lush gorgonians, reef fish, rainbow runners, horse-eye jacks, barracuda and occasionally sleeping nurse sharks.

52 CARACAS BAY LOST ANCHOR
★★★★★★★

Location: South coast, along the northwest wall of Caracas Bay
Access: By boat or shore
Conditions: Choppy with strong current
Average Depth: 20m (65ft)
Maximum Depth: 40m+ (130ft+)
Visibility: 30m (100ft)
This site features a heavy anchor chain that descends to well below sport diving limits. The dive profile is similar to that of Kabes di Baranka (Site 51). The drop-off is at 6m (20ft) and drops as an apparently never-ending wall of corals, lush gorgonians, reef fish and deep water fish.

53 TUGBOAT (TOWBOAT)
★★★★★★★★★

Location: South coast, off the protected southeast side of Caracas Bay
Access: By boat
Conditions: Normally calm, though around the southeast corner you are likely to hit strong and unpredictable currents
Average Depth: 5m (16ft)
Maximum Depth: 40m (130ft)
Visibility: 30m (100ft)
Another of Curaçao's top dives, this site includes a wreck that is small enough to be photographed in its entirety and a 45° sloping drop-off that begins in 9m (30ft) of water. The reef is packed with stony corals and gorgonian sea fans, sea rods and sea whips. In the shallow water, the tugboat rests upright on sand at 5m (15ft), carpeted with multi-coloured tube sponges and orange *Tubastrea* cup corals.

To the southeast of the tug the pretty, vertical wall is undercut in places and drops to about 30m (100ft) before shelving out at 45° or less. At the base of the wall there are large sheet corals. The tug attracts angelfish, trumpetfish, sergeant majors, chromis, groupers, snappers and moray eels. Along the wall, vase and basket sponges, black coral, lobsters, moray eels and scorpionfish are found. Be aware that around the southeast corner you are likely to hit strong and unpredictable currents.

54 KABAYE AND SMALL WALL
★★★★★★★★★

Location: South coast, just southeast of Caracas Bay by Directors Bay
Access: By boat
Conditions: Choppy with strong current
Average Depth: 20m (65ft)
Maximum Depth: 40m+ (130ft+)
Visibility: 30m (100ft)
Kabaye and Small Wall are next to each other and share similar diving. A mooring buoy, at 5m (15ft), marks the sites. A sandy terrace leads out from the shore and features staghorn and yellow pencil corals, octopuses, seahorses, sergeant majors, butterflyfish, angelfish and trumpetfish. The drop-off features star corals and lush gorgonians though the wall descends beyond sport diving depths. Two large sandy gullies intersect this wall and there are a number of nooks and crannies where moray eels, shrimps and lobsters hide.

55 PUNT'I PIKU/BARRACUDA POINT
★★★★★★

Location: South coast, across from Barbara Beach, near the mouth of Spanish Water (Spaanse Water)
Access: By boat
Conditions: Choppy with strong currents
Average Depth: 20m (65ft)
Maximum Depth: 40m (130ft)
Visibility: 30m (100ft)
This area has heavy boat traffic. The shallow water east of the buoy has elkhorn, staghorn, star and fire coral, large pillar corals and good gorgonian growth.

To seaward, east of the buoy, the drop-off is over 45°, beginning at about 9m (30ft) and continuing beyond 30m (100ft). The slope features large heads of mountainous star coral around 18m (60ft). To the west of the buoy, the drop-off is a wall descending to about 18m (60ft) before shelving off more gently. It is covered with gorgonians and sponges. The fish life includes barracuda, parrotfish, rainbow runners, horse-eye jacks, surgeonfish, damselfish, sergeant majors, grunts, snappers and Creole wrasse.

56 EEL VALLEY
★★★★★★★

Location: South coast, northwest end of Fuik Bay
Access: By boat
Conditions: Choppy with strong currents
Average Depth: 20m (65ft)
Maximum Depth: 40m (130ft)
Visibility: 30m (100ft)
Eel Valley has the usual sandy shallow plateau leading to a drop-off at 8m (25ft). It was originally named for its unusually high number of moray eels, though the numbers of these have now returned to normal. Staghorn corals are found in the shallows while leaf and star corals and gorgonians cover the drop-off, which descends to 30m (100ft) before shelving off deeper. There is an abundance of reef fish including squirrelfish, soldierfish, angelfish, foureye butterflyfish, trunkfish,

---

TURTLES AROUND THE ABC ISLANDS

Four species of sea turtles can be found around the ABC islands. In inshore waters you will often see green turtles (*Chelonia mydas*) that are herbivores and feed on sea-grass, and hawksbill turtles (*Eretmochelys imbricata*), which mostly feed on sponges. Loggerhead Turtles (*Caretta caretta*) and the massive leatherback turtles (*Dermochelys coriacea*) are more likely to be found offshore.

All sea turtles are on the endangered species list.

filefish, trumpetfish, damselfish, chromis, wrasse, parrotfish, goatfish, grunts, rainbow runners, snappers, barracuda, jacks and groupers.

57 NEWPORT
★★★★★★★

Location: South coast, offshore of Fuik Bay
Access: By boat
Conditions: Choppy with strong currents
Average Depth: 20m (65ft)
Maximum Depth: 40m (130ft)
Visibility: 30m (100ft)

Staghorn corals are found in the shallows here, while leaf and star corals and gorgonians cover the drop-off, which descends to 30m (100ft) before shelving off deeper. There is an abundance of reef fish including soldierfish, French angelfish, butterflyfish, porcupine pufferfish, scrawled filefish, trumpetfish, fusiliers, chromis, wrasse, parrotfish, goatfish, grunts, snappers, barracuda, jacks and groupers.

58 KATHY'S PARADISE
★★★★★★★

Location: South coast, southeast end of Fuik Bay, southeast of Nieuwpoort
Access: By boat
Conditions: Choppy with strong currents
Average Depth: 20m (65ft)
Maximum Depth: 40m (130ft)
Visibility: 30m (100ft)

Kathy's Paradise is the point that juts out from Nieuwpoort and therefore catches some rough seas. The strong currents produce a healthy reef life so it is a diver's paradise. Staghorn corals are found in the shallows, while leaf and star corals and gorgonians cover the drop-off, which descends to 30m (100ft) before shelving off deeper. Reef fish life is prolific and includes squirrelfish, soldierfish, angelfish, butterflyfish, trunkfish, filefish, trumpetfish, Creole wrasse, parrotfish, groupers and shoals of goatfish, grunts, snappers, barracuda and jacks.

59 SMOKEY/PUNT'I SANCHI
★★★★★★★

Location: South coast, offshore at the far eastern side of Fuik Bay
Access: By boat
Conditions: Choppy with strong currents and surge
Average Depth: 20m (65ft)
Maximum Depth: 40m (130ft)
Visibility: 30m (100ft)

Also called Punt'i Sanchi, Smokey has a wall seaward of the mooring buoy which begins at 6m (20ft) and drops to 30m (100ft). Above and on the drop-off there is healthy coral, sponge and gorgonian growth and the profuse fish life includes filefish, groupers, snappers, grunts, stingrays and eagle rays. This is a great dive.

60 GULIAUW
★★★★★★★

Location: South coast, east of Smokey (Site 59), west of Blanku Lagoon
Access: By boat
Conditions: Exposed, very choppy with strong currents
Average Depth: 20m (65ft)
Maximum Depth: 40m (130ft)
Visibility: 30m (100ft)

A very exposed dive, this is not for those who get seasick. It is best to fully kit-up before you leave the boat jetty, as the vessel will be rocking around when over the site. Snorkelling is only possible on the calmest days. Staghorn coral grows here at the unusually deep depth of 15m (50ft). The drop-off is at 8m (25ft) – above it there are fire and elkhorn corals, gorgonian sea fans, sea rods and sea whips. On the drop-off star, brain and pillar corals dominate and reef and pelagic fish thrive, including parrotfish, snappers, grunts, groupers, filefish, triggerfish, Creole wrasse, rainbow runners and horse-eye jacks.

61 PIEDRA PRETU/BLACK ROCK
★★★★

Location: Southeast coast, east of Blanku Lagoon
Access: By boat
Conditions: Very choppy with strong currents
Average Depth: 20m (65ft)
Maximum Depth: 40m+ (130ft+)
Visibility: 30m (100ft)

This site has a spectacular vertical wall but is subject to very rough seas. As with all these eastern sites it is more likely to be calmest in the early morning.

The mooring buoy is in 6m (20ft); to seaward the drop-off begins at 8m (25ft) and descends as a wall down to about 36m (120ft), before sloping off more gradually beyond depths to which sport divers should dive. The shallow plateau is covered with staghorn and elkhorn coral, large barrel sponges and gorgonians and the wall is covered with a dense forest of black coral. Near the base of the wall there are large disks of sheet corals. At around 25–27m (80–90ft) there are crevices filled with basslets, spotted morays and large green moray eels. The reef fish that feature here include parrotfish, surgeonfish, snappers, groupers, trumpetfish, goatfish and Creole wrasse.

Above: *Although slowly breaking up, the Tugboat (Site 53) remains an unusually picturesque wreck.*

62 NO WAY
★★★★

Location: Southeast coast, off the west of the large lagoon Awa di Oostpunt
Access: By boat
Conditions: Rough with strong currents
Average Depth: 20m (65ft)
Maximum Depth: 40m+ (130ft+)
Visibility: 30m (100ft)
No Way is so-called because of the rough, difficult conditions. However, despite this, it is one of the island's top dive sites and a visit is well worth the effort – though for experienced divers only. An old Spanish cannon in about 3m (10ft) gives the area its local fishermen's name 'Punt Canon'.

The mooring buoy is at about 8m (25ft); further out to sea the drop-off wall is near vertical and descends below sport diving depths. The shallow ledge has corals, sponges, gorgonians and green moray eels among its reef fish. A cave at about 24m (80ft) often has resting nurse sharks. Deeper down among the black corals there are pelagic species including rainbow runners, horse-eye jacks and barracuda as well as a multitude of reef fish, including squirrelfish, angelfish, butterflyfish, trunkfish,

filefish, trumpetfish, damselfish, chromis, fusiliers, Creole wrasse, parrotfish, goatfish, grunts and mahogany and schoolmaster snappers.

63 BASORA
★★★★

Location: Southeast coast, off the East Point of the island, by the entrance to the large lagoon Awa di Oostpunt
Access: By boat
Conditions: Very rough with seriously strong and changing currents
Average Depth: 20m (65ft)
Maximum Depth: 40m+ (130ft+)
Visibility: 30m (100ft)
Another challenging dive that is similar in profile to Piedra Pretu and No Way (sites 61–62). Above the drop-off the shallow ledge exhibits elkhorn and staghorn corals and luxuriant growth of gorgonian sea fans, sea rods, sea whips and sea plumes. The drop-off itself also has large black, brain, pillar and star corals. The fish here include large groupers, filefish, snappers, surgeonfish, Creole wrasse, moray eels, stingrays and many pelagic species.

Klein Curaçao is a tiny uninhabited island located 1½–2 hours by boat off the southeast of Curaçao. In good weather, excursions to the island are popular for sunbathing and beach parties, although there is no shade. The lighthouse is obsolete, and there are just a few fishermen's shacks, a jetty in poor repair on the leeward side and the hulk of a tanker aground on the windward side. When conditions are calm these sites are among Curaçao's top dives.

64 NORTHWEST CORNER
★★★★

Location: Off the northwest point
Access: By boat
Conditions: Can be rough with strong currents
Average Depth: 30m (100ft)
Maximum Depth: 40m (130ft)
Visibility: 30m (100ft)
At 30m (100ft), near the bottom of a steep wall, there is a large cave where there is the possibility of seeing sleeping nurse sharks (*Ginglymostoma cirratum*). The wall itself is covered with corals and has abundant fish life including large jewfish and other groupers, spotted and green moray eels, snappers, rainbow runners, jacks and barracuda. Turtles are often encountered.

Below: *A trumpetfish mimics a gorgonian sea whip for camouflage.*

65 NORTH OF THE MAIN BEACH AND

66 SOUTH OF THE MAIN BEACH
★★★★★★★★

Location: Either side of the main beach on the leeward side of Klein Curaçao
Access: By boat or shore
Conditions: Normally calm but some current and swell
Average Depth: 20m (65ft)
Maximum Depth: 40m+ (130ft+)
Visibility: 30m (100ft)
There are two dives on the leeward (southwest) side of the island, either side of the main beach. The drop-off on this side has some sand on it, so the coral is not so rich, but there are lots of reef fish, rainbow runners and moray eels hiding under coral heads. The reef fish include soldierfish, French and queen angelfish, banded and foureye butterflyfish, rock beauties, pufferfish, scrawled filefish, trumpetfish, damselfish, chromis, wrasse, parrotfish, goatfish, grunts, snappers and groupers.

67 DRIFT DIVE STARTING ON THE WINDWARD SIDE
★★★★

Location: The windward side of Klein Curaçao
Access: By boat
Conditions: Rough with strong currents
Average Depth: 20m (65ft)
Maximum Depth: 40m+ (130ft+)
Visibility: 30m (100ft)
When conditions permit, this is a spectacular dive. Divers are dropped in the rough seas on the windward side of the island and drift round to be picked up in the calm seas of the leeward side. A pretty wall drops to 30m (100ft), and is covered with orange elephant ear sponges, purple tube sponges, black corals, huge gorgonian sea fans and massive boulder corals, before shelving out further into the depths. Nooks and crannies shelter many invertebrates and the abundant fish life includes large pelagic species, moray eels, snappers, goatfish, stingrays, eagle rays, scorpionfish and occasionally sharks. Turtles are regularly encountered.

GETTING THERE

Hato International Airport is near to the Hato Caves, 11km (7 miles) north of the capital. Air connections are very good with Europe, the Americas and many parts of the Caribbean.

From Europe, KLM have regular daily services via Amsterdam from most major and many regional airports. TAP Air Portugal connect via Lisbon and British Airways via Miami or Caracas with connections on Curaçao's national carrier, ALM.

From North America there are direct flights from Atlanta, Chicago and New York though many flights connect via Miami with Air Aruba, ALM, American Airlines, Guyana Airways or United Airlines.

From Latin America there are regular services from Colombia, Guyana, Surinam, Venezuela and Central American countries.

From other Caribbean islands there are numerous connections with Aruba and Bonaire as well as the Windward Netherlands Antilles. Windward Islands Air International (WM) operates to Saba and St Eustatius. There are other connections to Cuba, the Dominican Republic, Haiti, Jamaica and Trinidad.

Airport tax is US$12.50 per person for international flights or US$5.65 for travel to other islands of the Netherlands Antilles. Children under two years old and passengers transiting within 24 hours are exempt.

Curaçao's port is located on the south coast at the capital, Willemstad. A major port of call on the itinerary of over 200 cruises from America and Europe, the Cruise Terminal is in the Otrobanda area of Willemstad. A ferry sails regularly between Venezuela and Curaçao.

WHERE TO STAY

Curaçao has more accommodation and facilities aimed at the European market than the other two ABC islands.

Apart from Habitat Curaçao, all other dive operators on Curaçao are concessions attached to hotels. Some of them do not have their own boats, but shore dive and hire a boat when they require one.

EXPENSIVE
Sonesta Beach Resort and Casino
Piscadera Bay; tel 599 9 7368800; fax 599 9 4627502

There are 248 rooms, three restaurants, all facilities and a casino. Caters for the disabled.

MID-RANGE
Coral Cliff Resort and Beach Club
Santa Martha Bay; tel 599 9 8641610; fax 599 9 8641781
There is the Cliff Hanger restaurant, a lounge and 35 rooms, most with kitchenettes. There is a complimentary daily shuttle service to Willemstad.

Curaçao Caribbean Hotel and Casino
PO Box 2133, Piscadera Bay; tel 599 9 625000; fax 599 9 625846
There are 181 rooms, five restaurants with themed nights and a casino.

Habitat Curaçao
Coral Estate, Rif St Marie; tel 599 9 8648800, USA 800 327 6709; fax 599 9 8648464; e-mail: curacao@habitatdiveresorts.com
A self-contained dive resort. More remote and private than most other resorts, it embraces the 'diving freedom' concept made famous at Captain Don's Habitat on Bonaire. There is a free daytime shuttle service to Willemstad.

Holiday Beach Hotel and Casino
PO Box 2178, Patere Euwensweg; tel 599 9 4625400, USA 800 44 5244; fax 599 9 46243979; e-mail: holbeach@cura.net
There are 200 rooms, two restaurants with themed nights and a casino. There is also a shuttle bus to Willemstad.

Lion's Dive Hotel and Marina
Bapor Kibrá; tel 599 9 4613100, USA 888 LIONS-DIVE; fax 599 9 4618200
There are 72 rooms and three restaurants. It is located just between Princess Beach Resort and the Curaçao Sea Aquarium.

Princess Beach Resort and Casino
Dr Martin Luther King Boulevard; tel 599 9 7367888, USA 800 332 8266; fax 599 9 4614131; e-mail: pbrsales@cura.net
A true mega-resort, this has everything. It is the largest resort on the island with 341 rooms and suites.

Van der Valk Plaza Hotel and Casino
PO Box 813, Plaza Pier, Willemstad; tel 599 9 4612500, USA 800 766 6016; fax 599 9 4616543; e-mail: info@plazahotelcuracao.com
A large resort with 235 rooms and 18 suites and an array of amenities including shops and a casino.

INEXPENSIVE
Airport Hotel Holland and Casino
524 Franklin D. Rooseveltweg; tel 599 9 8688044; fax 599 9 8688114
There are 46 rooms and a casino. It is convenient for the airport.

All West Apartments
Westpoint Beach; tel 599 9 8640102; fax 599 9 4612315; e-mail: allwest@cura.net
There are six apartments with kitchens or studios with kitchenettes.

Trupial Inn
5 Groot Davelaarweg; tel 599 9 7378200; fax 599 9 7371545
A cosy family hotel in a residential district. There are 74 rooms or suites with kitchenettes. There is also a sauna.

WHERE TO EAT

The restaurants in hotels or resorts are likely to be top class, but if you wish to try somewhere different the influence of so many different nationalities has meant that Curaçao offers a large choice of cuisine.

CARIBBEAN
Chez Suzenne
1 Blomonteweg; tel 599 9 8688545
Popular for local cuisine as Suzenne herself cooks the Curaçaon dishes.

Golden Star
2 Socratesstraat; tel 599 9 4654795
Typical West Indian restaurant on the corner of Dr Maalweg and Hugenholtzweg. Everything from meat, fish and hamburgers to egg-and-bacon sandwiches.

Oasis
79 Savonet, Banda Abou; tel 599 9 8640085
Local cuisine: goat stew, creole and seafood dishes.

Sombrero Room
Trupial Inn, 5 Groot Davelaarweg; tel 599 9 7378200
Local and international cuisine served in a 'Curaçao of the 1920's' setting.

CHINESE
Lam Yuen
25 Fokkerweg; tel 599 9 4615540
Healthy quantities of Chinese food.

Rose Garden
56 Oude Caracasbaaiweg; tel 599 9 4614574
Large helpings of Chinese food.

FRENCH
Grande-Café
18 Pietermaai; tel 599 9 4617077
French and local cuisine served in an easy-going atmosphere.

Larousse
5 Penstraat; tel 599 9 4655418
European-style restaurant for relaxed dining where French cuisine is served in the ambience of an 18th-century house. Fresh supplies are flown in from Holland.

INDIAN
Orient Express
Saliña Galleries; tel 599 9 4616203
Indian ambience and cuisine.

INDONESIAN
Garuda
Caribbean Hotel; tel 599 9 625000
Indonesian cuisine popular with the Dutch due to their past connections with Indonesia.

Rijsttafel Indonesia
13 Mercuriusstraat; tel 599 9 4612606
Serves Javanese specialities. The speciality of the house is a 16- or 25-dish rice table, served buffet style.

ITALIAN
Il Barile da Mario
Hanchi Snoa; tel 599 9 4613025
A bar and ristorante serving pasta, minestrone, seafood and fine wines. It is opposite the synagogue.

La Pergola
12 Waterfort Arches; tel 599 9 4613482
Fine Italian cuisine in the heart of town with good views. It is expensive.

INTERNATIONAL
Cliff Hanger Restaurant
Coral Cliff Resort & Beach Club; tel 599 9 8641610
Enjoy international cuisine while appreciating the fine view over the sea from the cliff.

De Taverne
Landhuise Groot Devalaar; tel 599 9 7370669
An old Curaçaon *landhuis*, furnished with antiques and lit with candles. Serves fish or large steak. It is very popular so reservations are requested.

Fort Nassau
tel 599 9 4613086
Local and international cuisine served in the pleasant ambience of an 18th-century fort. Good food and a fine view over St Anna Bay.

Fort Waakzaamheid
Berg Domi; tel 599 9 4623633
Local and international cuisine served in the ambience of an old fort that was captured by Bligh (the English captain of *The Bounty*). This restaurant is known for its value for money and has a good view over the town and harbour.

Oceans Bar and Restaurant
Habitat Curaçao, Coral Estate, Rif Santa Marie; tel 599 9 8648800
Popular with divers and local expatriates. Serves good local and international cuisine and there is a friendly service. Some nights are themed and/or have entertainment.

Rodeo Ranch
Curaçao Sea Aquarium; tel 599 9 4615757
Popular with divers as a meeting place. It serves international cuisine.

Rumours
Lions Dive Hotel & Marina, Bapor Kibrá; tel 599 9 4617555
Popular with divers as a meeting place. It serves international cuisine including meat and the fish catch of the day.

'T Kokkeltje
Airport Hotel Holland & Casino, 524 Franklin D. Rooseveltweg; tel 599 9 8688044
Dutch atmosphere with more than 15 types of fish or shellfish as well as steaks. Both local seafood and fish that is flown in from Holland. View over the airport runway.

MEXICAN
Margarita
Winkelcentrum Brievengate; tel 599 9 7372155
Authentic Mexican cuisine with a big 'Mariachi Night' on Fridays. Closed on Tuesdays.

DIVE FACILITIES

Apart from Habitat Curaçao, all other dive operators on Curaçao are concessionary operators attached to hotels. Some operators do not have their own boats but will hire one if required.

All West Diving & Adventures Curaçao
West Point Beach; tel 599 9 8640102; fax 599 9 4612315; e-mail: allwest@cura.net
Training up to Open Water Diver level offered in Dutch, English and German.

Aqua Diving
4 Martha Koosje, Weg van Westpunt; tel 599 9 8649700; fax 599 9 8649288; e-mail: dive@aquadiving.com

Specializes in shore diving. Training up to Assistant Instructor level offered in Dutch, English, German and Spanish.

Atlantis Diving I
6 Drielstraat; tel 599 9 4658288; fax 599 9 4658288; e-mail: diving@cura.net
Training up to Instructor level offered in Dutch, English, German, Papiamento, Portuguese and Spanish.

Atlantis Diving II
PO Box 6121, John F. Kennedy Boulevard; tel 599 9 4626200; fax 599 9 4628099; e-mail: atlantis@cura.net
On the beach between the Sonesta and the Caribbean Hotels. Training up to Instructor level offered in Dutch, English, German, Papiamento, Portuguese and Spanish.

Big Blue Diving
Club Seru Coral, 10 Koraal Partier; tel 599 9 8642822; fax 599 9 8642237
Associated with Hotel Club Seru Coral. Training offered up to Assistant Instructor level.

Caribbean Sea Sports N.V.
Sonesta Hotel, John F. Kennedy Boulevard, Piscadera Bay; tel 599 9 7368800; fax 599 9 4626933; e-mail: css@cura.net
PADI instruction in conjunction with the Sonesta Hotel.

Curaçao Seascape
PO Box 2133, Curaçao Caribbean Hotel & Casino; tel 599 9 625000; fax 599 9 625846; e-mail: montoo@ibm.net
Established for 30 years, originally as Piscadera. Courses up to Divemaster level offered in Dutch, English, French and German.

Diving School Wederfoort/Sami Scuba Center
93 Bocaweg; tel 599 9 8684414; fax 599 9 8692062; e-mail: duiweder@cura.net
Long established, associated with several hotels and apartments. Courses offered up to Assistant Instructor level.

Dolphin Divers Curaçao
91 Diamarie, Las Palmas Beach; tel 599 9 4628180; fax 599 9 4628181
Associated with the Las Palmas Hotel. Instruction is based on PADI or German standards.

Easy Divers Curaçao
Coral Cliff Hotel, Santa Martha Bay; tel/fax 599 9 8642822; e-mail: easydivers@curinfo.an

Beside Santa Martha Bay with courses on Nitrox and up to Assistant Instructor level offered in Dutch, English and German.

Eden Roc Diving Center
c/o Holiday Beach Hotel & Casino, Patere Euwensweg; tel/fax 599 9 4628878; cellular: 5605690; e-mail: edenroc@ibm.net
A PADI 5-Star Instructor Development Center based on the beach at the Holiday Beach Hotel. Instruction offered in Dutch, English and German.

Habitat Curaçao Dive Resort
Coral Estate, Rif Santa Marie; tel 599 9 8648800, USA 800 327 6790; fax 599 9 8648464; e-mail: curacao@habitatdiveresorts.com
A PADI 5-Star Instructor Development Center teaching in Dutch, English, German, Papiamento and Spanish. Nitrox courses are available as is photo and video instruction by Chris Richards. Voted by American Divers as among the top fifteen dive resorts worldwide and tied third as the best dive operator in the Caribbean, Habitat Curaçao believe in total diving freedom. Their staff are not there to dictate how you dive but to assist and advise. Three boat dives are offered as standard each day plus unlimited shore diving; full diving cylinders are available 24 hours a day.

Holland Diving Curaçao
Airport Hotel Holland & Casino, 524 Franklin D. Rooseveltweg; tel 599 9 8697060; fax 599 9 8697060
Located at Hotel Holland with training offered up to Instructor level.

Kunuku Pension Dive IN N.V.
1 Hansje; tel 599 9 8642572; fax 599 9 8642578
Accommodation in a refurbished 'Kunuku' farmhouse. Training offered up to Divemaster level.

Ocean Divers Curaçao
15B Socratesstraat; tel 599 9 4657254; fax 599 9 4657254
PADI training offered up to Assistant Instructor level.

Princess Divers
Princess Beach Resort & Casino, 8 Dr Martin Luther King Boulevard; tel 599 9 4658991, USA 800 9 DANCER; fax 599 9 4655756; e-mail: dancer@peterhughes.com
This is a Peter Hughes PADI 5-Star facility based at the Princess Beach Resort. Nitrox and Nitrox courses are available.

Scuba Do Dive Center
Jan Thiel Beach & Sports Resort; tel 599 9 7679300; fax 599 9 7679300

Training up to Assistant Instructor level offered in Dutch, English, French, German and Spanish.

Silent Immersion N.V.
6 Drielstraat; tel 599 9 4651575; fax 599 9 4658288; e-mail: silent@cura.net
Offers deep exploration of various dive sites, as well as Nitrox, Rebreather and Trimix technical diving instruction.

Toucan Diving
Van der Valk Plaza Hotel & Casino, Plaza Pier, PO Box 813; tel 599 9 4612500, USA 800 766 6016; fax 599 9 4616543; e-mail: info@plazahotelcuracao.com
IDD Instructor Development Centre with training up to Instructor level offered in Dutch, English and German.

The Ultimate Dive Store
23 Orionweg; tel 599 9 7379487; fax 599 9 7368169
Diver training up to Assistant Instructor level offered in Dutch, English and German.

Underwater Curaçao
Lions Dive Hotel & Marina, Bapor Kibrá; tel 599 9 4618100; fax 599 9 4618200; e-mail: lionsdive@ibm.net
A PADI Instructor Development Center. Training offered in Dutch, English, German, Papiamento and Spanish. It is beside the Sea Aquarium.

FILM PROCESSING

There are various film processing facilities on Curaçao.

Fotostudio Tram
36 Dr. Hugenholtzweg, tel 599 9 4613487 Promenade Winkelcentrum, tel 599 9 7376535
Winkelcentrum Colon, tel 599 9 4626747

Habitat Curaçao Dive Resort
Coral Estate, Rif Santa Marie; tel 599 9 8648800

Interphoto CV
Dokweg z/n, tel 599 9 7376263

Princess Divers
Princess Beach Resort & Casino, Dr. Martin Luther King Boulevard; tel 599 9 4658991
E6 processing only

Samson Curaçao N.V.
Fuji image Plaza, 23 Hanchi di Snoa; tel 599 9 4611370
Jan Noordweg z/n, tel 599 9 8691443
Unit D 101/102, Salinja Galleries; tel 599 9 4652655

Studio Kort
169 Winston Churchillweg; tel 599 9 8690562

Toucan Diving
Van der Valk Plaza Hotel & Casino, Plaza Pier; tel 599 9 4612500

RECOMPRESSION CHAMBER

The 750-bed St Elisabeth Hospital (St Elisabeth Gasthuis) is one of the largest and most up to date in the Caribbean. It is located in Willemstad's Otrobanda district and contains the island's two hyperbaric chambers.

St Elizabeth Hospital, tel 599 9 4625100/4624900
Recompression Chamber, tel 599 9 4637457/4637288

EMERGENCIES

Curaçao Emergency Telephone Numbers:

Ambulance	112
Fire Department	114
Hospital	110
Police	114
Tourism Security Assistance	4617991

USEFUL CONTACTS

Visit Curaçao's main web site: http://www.interknowledge.com/curacao

Curaçao Tourism Development Bureau
19 Pietermaai, PO Box 3266, Willemstad, Curaçao, Netherlands Antilles; tel 599 9 4616000; fax 599 9 461-2305; e-mail: ctdbcur@ibm.net

Curaçao Tourism Development Bureau UK
Axis Sales & Marketing Ltd., 421a Finchley Road, London NW3 6HJ; tel 020 74314045; fax 020 74317920; e-mail: destinations@pwaxis.co.uk

Curaçao Tourist Bureau Europe
82-84 Vastland, 3011 BP Rotterdam, Holland; tel (010) 414 2639; e-mail: ctbenl@wirehub.nl

The Curaçao Tourist Board – Miami
330 Biscayne Boulevard, Suite 808, Miami, FL 33132; tel (305) 3745811; 800 445 8266; fax (305) 3746741

The Curaçao Tourist Board – New York
475 Park Avenue South, Suite 2000, New York, NY 10016; tel: (212) 683-7660; 800 Curaçao; fax: (212) 683-9337; e-mail: curacao@ix.netcom.com

Lizardfish/sand diver (family Synodontidae)
Lizardfish are named after their lizard-like heads. They
lie motionless and camouflaged on the bottom waiting
for prey to swim by. They will not move even if you
approach closely with a camera.

Lizardfish/sand diver, 20–45cm (8–18in), *Synodus intermedius*

Moray eels (family Muraenidae)
This ancient family of fish have gained their undeserved
reputation for ferocity largely because, as they breathe,
they open and close the mouth to reveal their numerous sharp teeth. They do not have fins or scales. Moray
eels hide the rear portion of their bodies in a selected
coral crevice and are fairly inactive during the day. They
emerge at night to feed.

Spotted moray eel, 45–90cm (18–36in), *Gymnothorax moringa*

Parrotfish (family Scaridae)
So-called because of their sharp, parrot-like beaks and
bright colours, parrotfish are among the most important herbivores on the reef. Many change colour and
sex as they grow. The terminal-phase males develop
striking coloration in comparison with the drab initial-
phase males and females. These fish consume consider-
able amounts of coral limestone when feeding.

Redband parrotfish, 18–28cm (7–11in), *Sparisoma aurofrenatum*

Pufferfish/balloonfish/burrfish (family
Tetraodontidae)
These small to medium-size omnivores feed on algae,
worms, molluscs and crustaceans. Pufferfish are found
all the way down the reef to depths of around 30m
(100ft). They are slow moving but when threatened,
they inflate themselves into big, round balls by sucking
water into the abdomen, so that it becomes almost an
impossible task for predators to swallow them.

Porcupine pufferfish, 30–90cm (12–36in), *Diodon hystrix*

Soapfish (family Grammistidae)
Named after a toxic, soap-like mucus that they secrete,
soapfish are the height of inactivity, often resting on
the bottom or leaning against ledges. They are so lazy
that divers can approach them closely. Soapfish hunt
at night.

Greater soapfish, 13–33cm (5–13in), *Rypticus saponaceus*

OTHER FISH AND INVERTEBRATES

Anemones (phylum Cnidaria, order Actiniaria)
Sea anemones come in many different shapes and sizes. Their tentacles have stinging nematocysts that paralyse any small fish or invertebrates that brush against them and then draw the prey to the mouth at the centre of the anemone's disc. Some species of crab, shrimp and fish can live in symbiosis with anemones without being stung by the nematocysts. Anemones can move slowly and will fight other anemones nearby; they can also retract their tentacles for protection.

Angelfish (family Pomacanthidae)
A close relative of the butterflyfish and equally as beautiful, angelfish browse on sponges, algae and corals using their minute, brush-like teeth. Their vibrant colouring varies according to the species, like those of the butterflyfish and they were once thought part of the same family. However, they are distinguishable by a short spike extending from the gill cover. Angelfish are territorial in habit and tend to occupy the same caves or ledges for a period of time. Large angelfish species produce loud a drumming noise when agitated.

Barracuda (family Sphyraenidae)
With their elongated silvery body and sinister-looking jaws, barracuda look rather fearsome. Though they rarely threaten divers (but have a habit of following them about), it is wise to approach large, lone individuals with caution. Barracuda are effective reef predators; they tend to school when young, but hunt singly or in pairs when mature.

Bigeyes (family Priacanthidae)
As their name suggests, these small, nocturnal fish have large eyes. Effective predators, they hover in holes in the reef or under overhangs during the day and venture further afield to feed at night.

Butterflyfish (family Chaetodontidae)
Among the most colourful of reef inhabitants, butterflyfish have compressed, thin bodies, usually with a stripe through the eye and sometimes with a dark blotch near the tail: this serves as camouflage and confuses predators, who lunge for the wrong end of the fish. Butterflyfish can also swim backwards to escape danger. Many species live as mated pairs and have territories.

Calcareous tube worms (phylum Annelida, family Serpulidae)
Divers easily notice Christmas tree worms because of their colour and beauty. They live in calcareous tubes embedded in live corals, the two fan-shaped spiral whorls, called radioles, protrude from the tubes with a sharp spine above the mouth. The worms withdraw instantly when approached and a hard structure called an operculum closes over the tube opening.

Cardinalfish (family Apogonidae)
The nocturnal counterpart of the damselfish in terms of sheer abundance, at night cardinalfish actively feed on small shrimps and crabs. In some species the males incubate the eggs inside their mouths.

Crabs (phylum Crustacea, order Decapoda)
Crabs have evolved reduced abdomens and tails. The first pair of legs have grown claws that are used for fighting or posturing and the manipulation of objects such as when feeding. The other four pairs of legs enable the animal to rapidly move sideways. Most species are small and prefer to remain hidden. Some such as the yellowline arrow crab usually only come out at night.

Feather stars (phylum Echinodermata, class Crinoidea)
Often referred to as 'living fossils' as they have changed little according to fossil records, feather stars have bodies with five arms that divide to give them long arms in multiples of five. Numerous short appendages cover each arm to give a feather-like appearance and catch passing food in the current. These arms adhere tightly to anything that comes into contact with them and are said to be the original idea behind Velcro. As with sea stars the arms can regenerate if broken off. Some crinoids can swim short distances but they usually walk on short jointed legs called cirri.

Flounders (family Bothidae)
Flounders are flatfish that lie on their sides – within weeks of birth, the eye on the underside migrates to the exposed side and the exposed pectoral fin acts like a dorsal fin. Flounders can change their colour to blend in with the bottom and partially bury themselves in the sand or mud. They glide over the seabed with an undulating motion. The peacock flounder has blue spots and the unusually long exposed pectoral fin is often erect while the fish is swimming.

Goatfish (family Mullidae)
Bottom dwellers, goatfish are easily recognized by a pair of barbels under their chin, which they use to rummage in the sand for prey. They are usually found in small groups or large shoals.

Gobies (family Gobiidae)
The goby is a 'bottom dweller' and has the ability to remain stationary and undetected on the seabed for long periods of time. They have large protruding eyes, which are raised above the level of the head, and powerful jaws which enable them to snatch prey and dart back to safety. The goby family is one of the most successful, with literally hundreds of species. In fact new species of these small, secretive fish are being discovered all the time.

Gorgonians (phylum Cnidaria, order Gorgonacea)
Gorgonians is the preferred name for the octocorals that are often mistakenly called 'soft corals' by Caribbean dive masters because they are flexible and often appear bushy. Gorgonians include sea fans, sea plumes, sea rods and sea whips. Sea fans are always set perpendicular to the current so that their polyps, which are so close together as to be almost touching, can efficiently sieve the current for food.

Jacks, palometas, permits and **rainbow runners** (family Carangidae)
Jacks are open water (pelagic) fish, though shoals often pass over reefs while following the current in search of prey. A few species find it productive to remain near reefs, such as horse-eye jacks, palometa and permits. Cruising outer reef slopes, they dash in to catch unwary prey. They are usually in small groups but are sometimes seen in large shoals.

Sea cucumbers (phylum Echinodermata, class Holothuroidea)
Sea cucumbers are sausage-shaped with a mouth at one end and an anus at the other. Like other echinoderms they have a water-vascular system, which operates their tube-feet by hydraulic pressure. The skeletons of sea cucumbers consist of small spicules within their leathery body-wall. Taking in sediment through the mouth as they crawl across the reef, extracting organic debris and voiding the waste sand through their anus, they shift large amounts of sand.

Soldierfish and **squirrelfish** (family Holocentridae)
These are predominantly red fish that hide under overhangs or in crevices during the day and come out to feed at night.

Snappers (family Lutjanidae)
They are called snappers because they snap their jaws when hooked on a line. Snappers are often associated with grunts, but snappers have prominent canine teeth while grunts do not. Snappers are nocturnal predators that hang around singly or in small groups during the day.

Sponges (phylum Porifera)
The basic sponge structure is made up of a collection of cells that enclose canals and chambers that open to the outside and inside through pores. The form is supported by a skeleton of calcareous or siliceous spicules and a matrix of fibres. Water is drawn through the outer pores and as it passes through the canals, food and oxygen are filtered out. The water exits into the sponge's interior cavity and out through its excurrent openings. Sponges are responsible for much of the colour visible on Caribbean reefs.

Surgeonfish (family Acanthuridae)
Grazers of algae, surgeonfish have spines like scalpels at the base of their tails. They can be solitary but often shoal in large groups.

Triggerfish (family Balistidae)
These medium to large fish, with flattened bodies and powerful teeth, feed on crustaceans and echinoderms on the mid-reef. When a triggerfish is threatened it squeezes itself into a crevice and erects its first dorsal spine. Locking it into place with a second, smaller spine, this first dorsal spine stays wedged until the 'trigger' is released.

Trumpetfish (family Aulostomidae)
Expert at changing colour to blend in with a background, trumpetfish are always solitary. They often hide among branching corals or gorgonian sea rods, lining up their bodies with the branches even if they are vertical. They closely shadow fish such as pufferfish to sneak up on prey.

Tunicates/sea squirts (phylum Chordata, class Ascidiacea)
Tunicates, also called sea squirts, come in many colours and are often translucent. Their habit of filtering food is similar to that of sponges but when disturbed they can close their siphons quickly. Solitary tunicates are called simple ascidians, while those that exist as colonies of many individuals are called compound tunicates. Some species are only joined at their bases while others are completely embedded in a common tunic. In some species their excurrent siphons open into a single, shared chamber.

Yellowfin mojarras (family Gerreidae)
Yellowfin mojarras swim slowly or hover over the sand and dig for small invertebrates.

Wrasse/hogfish (family Labridae)
This is a colourful and conspicuous group of fish, easily recognized by shape and the bird-like way of swimming. Most wrasse constantly move about and can change sex from female to male.

Underwater Photography and Video

Underwater photography requires a good deal of preparation before entering the water. You cannot change prime lenses underwater, so it's important to establish what you wish to photograph before you take the plunge, in order to get the best results. There is the possibility of using a zoom lens on a housed camera or a Nikonos RS-AF, which gives a degree of extra flexibility, but zoom lenses can lack sharpness. If the water is calm you can carry two camera outfits, one for wide-angle and another for close-up or macro.

DEDICATED UNDERWATER CAMERAS

The Nikonos V and the Sea & Sea Motor Marine II are both non-reflex waterproof cameras with Through-The-Lens (TTL) automatic exposure systems with dedicated flash guns. In stronger currents the Nikonos V is easier to handle. Nikonos lenses range from 15mm to 80mm in focal length: the 35mm and 80mm lenses can be used in air, and are really only useful underwater when fitted to extension tubes or close-up outfits; the 28mm lens should be considered as the standard lens.

Independent companies supply lenses, lens converters, extension tubes and a housing for fish-eye and superwide land camera lenses to fit the Nikonos. Lens converters are particularly convenient as they can be changed underwater. The Motor Marine II, for example, makes good use of these, with converters for wide-angle and macro. The Nikonos close-up kit can also be changed underwater. The specially designed Nikonos lenses give sharper results underwater than any housed lenses, though the lack of reflex focusing makes it difficult to compose pictures and it is easy to cut off part of a subject. Remember that the focusing scale on the 35mm and 80mm is inscribed in 'in-air' distances, while that on the 15mm, 20mm and 28mm underwater lenses is inscribed in underwater distances.

The now-discontinued Nikonos RS-AF is a fully waterproof reflex camera with autofocus, dedicated lenses and a dedicated flash gun. It is very heavy. Its high price makes it a poor buy in comparison with housed high-specification land cameras, which are more versatile, weigh less, are cheaper to replace when flooded and can be used on land.

HOUSED CAMERAS

Land cameras can be used underwater in specialist metal or Plexiglas housings. These are available for top-grade reflex cameras. There are advantages and disadvantages to each system. Metal housings are strong, reliable, work well at depth and will last a long time if properly maintained. However, they can be heavy to carry – though they do have buoyancy in water. Their higher cost is justified if one is using an expensive camera that deserves the extra protection.

Plexiglas housings are cheaper but more fragile and require careful handling, both above and below the water. Some models compress at depth, making the control rods miss the camera controls. These control rods can be adjusted to work at depths, but then do not function properly near the surface. Most underwater photographs are taken near to the surface, so this drawback is not serious. These housings are lightweight to carry on land, but often too buoyant in the water where you have to attach extra weights to them.

'O' Rings and Other Equipment

Underwater cameras, housings, flash guns and cables have 'O' ring seals. These and their mating surfaces or grooves must be kept scrupulously clean. 'O' rings should be lightly greased with silicone grease to prevent flooding (the Nikonos RS-AF uses a different grease). Too much grease will attract grit and hairs. Silicone spray should not be used, as its cooling effect causes 'O' rings to crack. When not in use, it is best to store any user-removable 'O' rings off the unit to avoid them becoming flattened. The unit itself should then be sealed in a plastic bag to keep out moisture. User-removable 'O' rings on Nikonos cameras and flash synchronization cables are best replaced every 12 months. Non-user-removable 'O' rings should be serviced every 12–18 months. As a general rule, those on housings usually last the life of the housing.

Note that housings without controls, which are designed for fully auto cameras, require fast films to obtain reasonable shutter speeds and lens apertures in the low ambient light underwater. Autofocus systems that

---

THE ADVANCED PHOTO SYSTEM

Some SLRs and compact cameras (but not the Nikonos or Sea & Sea) are available in the Advanced Photo System (APS). APS has fool-proof drop-in film cassettes; you do not have to thread the film or rewind it, and processed film remains in the cassette for protection. Cassettes have symbols indicating whether the film is unexposed, partially exposed, or fully exposed or whether they have been processed. Fully exposed or processed films are automatically rejected and the camera cannot be opened unless the film is rewound. With higher specification cameras, the film can be rewound and changed mid-film in air.

Three image formats are possible in-camera on the same film: 'C', Classic has the standard 2:3 aspect ratio; 'H', HDTV for group and wide shots has a 9:16 aspect ratio; and 'P', Panoramic has a 1:3 aspect ratio.

A magnetic strip on the film records the selected picture size, and APS processing equipment uses this data to make frame-by-frame adjustments to optimize each photograph.

work on contrast (not infrared) work underwater but only on high contrast subjects – not on those that have large areas of one colour. When balancing flash with daylight, cameras with faster flash synchronization speeds, 1/125 or 1/250 second, give sharper results by avoiding the double images associated with fast moving fish.

Masks hold your eyes away from the viewfinder, so buy the smallest volume mask you can wear. Cameras fitted with optical action finders or eyepiece magnifiers are useful in housings but this is not so important with auto-focus systems.

Light refraction through your mask and through the camera lens causes objects to appear one-third closer and larger than in air. Reflex focusing or visually estimated distances remain correct, but if you measure distances by a ruler, these must be reduced by one-third when setting the lens focus if it is inscribed in 'in-air' distances.

With a flat port (window), in front of the lens, refraction increases the focal length of the lens and decreases its sharpness, due to the individual colours of light being refracted at different angles and speeds (chromatic aberration). This is most pronounced with wide-angle lenses, which should be corrected by using a convex dome port. Dome ports require lenses to be able to focus on a virtual image at around 30cm (1ft), so you may have to fit supplementary positive dioptre lenses to some camera lenses.

FLASH

Water acts as a cyan (blue/green) filter, cutting back red, so colour film will have a blue/green cast. For available light photography, different filters are sold to correct this in either cold or tropical waters, but they reduce the already limited amount of light available. Flash will put back the colour and increase apparent sharpness.

Modern flash guns have TTL automatic exposure systems. Underwater, large flash guns have good wide-angle performance usable up to 1.5m (5ft). Smaller flash guns have a narrow angle and only work up to 1m (40 inches) – diffusers widen the angle covered, but you lose at least one F-stop in output. Some land flash guns are more advanced than most underwater flash guns, and can be housed for underwater use.

Flash guns used on or near to the camera will light up suspended matter in the water like white stars in a black sky (back scatter). The closer these particles are to the camera, the larger they will appear. The solution is to keep the flash as far as possible above and to one side of the camera. Two narrow-angle flash guns, one on each side of the camera, often produce a better result than a single wide-angle flash gun.

When photographing divers, remember the golden rule that the eyes within the mask must be lit and in focus. Flash guns with a colour temperature of 4500° Kelvin will give more accurate skin tones and colour.

In a multiple flash set-up the prime flash gun will meter by TTL if this is available and (unless it has TTL-Slave) any other flash gun connected will give its pre-programmed output, so this should be set low to achieve

modelling light. TTL-Slaves should have a lower output than the main flash for the same reason.

Multiple segment matrix flash exists with some housed cameras connected to housed matrix flash guns. With other TTL systems, although the ambient light metering may be multiple segment matrix, the flash metering is by a single segment in the centre of the frame. This means that flash on smaller off-centre foreground subjects may not be correctly metered with these systems.

Although objects appear closer to both your eye and the camera lens under water, the flash must strike the subject directly to illuminate it. Narrow-angle flash guns must therefore be aimed behind the apparent subject, to hit the real subject. Built-in aiming/focusing lights, or a torch strapped to the flash, aid both this problem and focusing during night photography. Built-in aiming/focusing lights are best powered by a separate battery, or the system will not last for a complete dive.

Fish scales reflect light in different ways that vary with the angle of the fish to the camera. Silver fish reflect more light than coloured fish and black fish almost none at all – therefore you should bracket exposures. With automatic flash guns you do this by altering the film speed setting.

The easiest way to balance flash with available light is to use TTL flash with a camera on aperture priority metering. Take a meter reading of the mid-water background that agrees with your chosen flash synchronization speed, set your flash to TTL and it will correctly light your subject. If you do not have multi-segment matrix flash then your subject should be in the central part of the frame. If you use manual exposure, using an aperture half a stop higher than the meter recommends will give a darker background and make the subject stand out more.

If possible bracket your exposures by altering the film speed. At distances of less than 1m (40 inches) most automatic flash guns tend to overexpose so you must allow for this. Once you have learnt the correct exposures for different situations you can begin experimenting with manual exposure for creativity.

FILM

For black and white photography, fast 400 ISO film is the first choice. For a beginner wishing to use colour, negative print film is best, offering plenty of exposure latitude. Reversal film is preferred for reproduction, but requires very accurate exposure.

Kodachrome films are ideal for close work but with mid-water shots they produce a blue/green water background – although this is accurate, people are conditioned to a 'blue' sea. Ektachrome and Fujichrome produce blue water backgrounds; 50–100 ISO films are the best compromise between exposures and grain. Pale yellow filters will cut down the blue.

Kodak's Underwater Ektachrome would be very useful for coral and large subjects such as shipwrecks, whale sharks and manta rays if only it had a film speed of 200 ISO or greater. As it is, with a film speed of 50 ISO, its uses are limited in the low light levels prevalent underwater.

Push/Pull Processing

Colour negative films have an exposure latitude of up to four stops and black-and-white films have even more, but colour transparency films should be exposed to within a quarter of a stop of the correct value.

If you have been on holiday or on a longer trip there is always the possibility that cameras, flash guns and meters have not behaved correctly. Processors anywhere can suffer problems from power cuts or machinery failure, so professional photographers never have all their exposed film processed at the same time; instead they process it in small batches. This has the advantage that you can review the results of the films processed. If all is not right, E6 process films can have their processing adjusted by professional processing laboratories, who can 'push' them by up to two stops faster or 'pull' them back by one stop slower. There will be some change in colour and contrast but not a lot.

Kodachrome film can be adjusted to a lesser extent by laboratories in the USA or Kodak's Professional Laboratory at Wimbledon in the UK.

If you have any doubts about a particular film you can have a 'clip test' done; the first few frames are cut off and processed separately first, then the rest of the film is processed according to the results of the clip test.

PHOTOGRAPHIC SUBJECTS

What you photograph depends on your personal interests. Macro photography with extension tubes and fixed framers is easiest to get right: the lens-to-subject distance and flash-to-subject distance are fixed, and the water sediment is minimized. Expose a test film at a variety of exposures with a fixed set-up and the best result will be the exposure to use for all future pictures for this setting and film.

Some fish are strongly territorial. Surgeonfish, triggerfish and sharks will make mock attacks on a perceived invader and these situations can make strong pictures if you are brave enough to hold your ground. Manta rays are curious and will keep coming back if you react quietly and do not chase after them. Angelfish and butterflyfish will swim off when you first enter their territory, but if you remain quietly in the same place they will usually return and allow you to photograph them. Remember that if an eye is in the picture it must be lit and sharp, it is acceptable for the rest of the animal to be slightly blurred.

FILM AND CONDENSATION

Keep film in its individual sealed containers until you use it.

If you must buy film locally, buy it in a respected photography outlet or major hotel, where it will have spent most of its storage life in cool conditions.

If you keep film refrigerated, give it at least two hours to defrost before loading it in a camera.

Do not assemble underwater cameras or housings in cool air-conditioned rooms or cabins; you are likely to get condensation inside them when you then take them into the water.

Normal cameras that have been in air-conditioned rooms, cabins or vehicles will mist up when taken out into a warm atmosphere. You will have to wait at least ten minutes for the condensation to evaporate before you can take any clear photographs.

Diver and wreck photography are the most difficult. Even with apparently clear water and wide-angle lenses there will be back scatter, and flash is essential to light a diver's mask. Note that when the sun is at a low angle, or in choppy seas, much of the light fails to enter the water. To take advantage of the maximum light available it is best to photograph two hours either side of the sun's highest point. Sunlight can give spectacular effects underwater, especially in silhouette shots, though generally you should keep the sun behind you and on your subject.

Night photography underwater is another world. Focusing quickly in dim light is difficult and many subjects will disappear when lit up, so pre-set the controls. Many creatures only appear at night and some fish are half asleep, making them more approachable.

For all kinds of photography, good buoyancy control is essential. Remember not to touch coral and do not wear fins over sandy bottoms, as they will stir sand up.

VIDEO

If underwater photography sounds too difficult, try video. Macro subjects require extra lighting but other shots can be taken with available light and if necessary improved electronically afterwards. Back scatter is much less of a problem and the results can be played back on site and shot again if necessary or the tape can be used again.

Batteries

A major problem for travelling photographers and videographers alike is keeping up with battery charging. If your equipment can use AA or D cell batteries, these will be available at most mainland towns, though they may be old or stored in bad conditions. If you can carry the weight it is best to take a fresh supply with you.

Despite their memory problems, rechargeable nickel cadmium batteries have advantages in cold weather – they recharge flash guns much more quickly and can usually be used again if flooded. Make sure that you carry spares and have chargers of the correct voltage and Hertz for your destination. Most video cameras and many flash guns have dedicated battery packs, so carry at least one spare and keep it charged.

Health and Safety for Divers

The information on first aid and safety in this part of the book is intended as a guide only. It is based on currently accepted health and safety guidelines, but it is merely a summary and is no substitute for a comprehensive manual on the subject – or, even better, for first aid training. We strongly advise you to buy a recognized manual on diving safety and medicine before setting off on a diving trip, to read it through during the journey, and to carry it with you to refer to during the trip. It would also be sensible to take a short course in first aid.

We urge anyone in need of advice on emergency treatment to see a doctor as soon as possible.

WHAT TO DO IN AN EMERGENCY
- Divers who have suffered any injury or symptom of an injury, no matter how minor, related to diving, should consult a doctor, preferably a specialist in diving medicine, as soon as possible after the symptom or injury occurs.
- No matter how confident you are in making a diagnosis, remember that you are an amateur diver and an unqualified medical practitioner.
- If you are the victim of a diving injury do not let fear of ridicule prevent you from revealing your symptoms. Apparently minor symptoms can mask or even develop into a life-threatening illness. It is better to be honest with yourself and live to dive another day.
- Always err on the conservative side when treating an illness or an injury. If you find that the condition is only minor you – and the doctor – will both be relieved.

FIRST AID
The basic principles of first aid are to:
- do no harm
- sustain life
- prevent deterioration
- promote recovery.

If you have to treat an ill or injured person:
- First try to secure the safety of yourself and the ill or injured person by getting the two of you out of the threatening environment: the water.
- Think before you act: do not do anything that will further endanger either of you.
- Then follow a simple sequence of patient assessment and management:
  1 Assess whether you are dealing with a life-threatening condition.
  2 If so, try to define which one.
  3 Then try to manage the condition.

Assessing the ABCs:
Learn the basic checks – the ABCs:
A: for AIRWAY (with care of the neck)
B : for BREATHING
C: for CIRCULATION
D: for DECREASED level of consciousness
E: for EXPOSURE (a patient must be exposed enough for a proper examination to be made).

- **Airway (with attention to the neck):** check whether the patient has a neck injury. Are the mouth and nose free from obstruction? Noisy breathing is a sign of airway obstruction.

- **Breathing:** look at the chest to see if it is rising and falling. Listen for air movement at the nose and mouth. Feel for the movement of air against your cheek.

- **Circulation:** feel for a pulse (the carotid artery) next to the windpipe.

- **Decreased level of consciousness:** does the patient respond in any of the following ways?
  A - Awake, aware, spontaneous speech.
  V - Verbal stimuli: does he or she answer to 'Wake up'?
  P - Painful stimuli: does he or she respond to a pinch?
  U - Unresponsive.

- **Exposure:** preserve the dignity of the patient as much as you can, but remove clothes as necessary to carry out your treatment.

Now, send for help
If, after your assessment, you think the condition of the patient is serious, you must send or call for help from the nearest emergency services (ambulance, paramedics). Tell whoever you send for help to come back and let you know whether help is on the way.

Recovery position
If the patient is unconscious but breathing normally there is a risk that he or he she may vomit and choke on the vomit. It is therefore critical that the patient be turned on one side into the recovery position. This is illustrated in all first aid manuals.

If you suspect injury to the spine or neck, immobilize the patient in a straight line before you turn him or her on one side.

If the patient is unconscious, does not seem to be breathing, and you cannot feel a pulse, do not try to turn him or her into the recovery position.

Do **NOT** give fluids to unconscious or semi-conscious divers.

Hyperthermia (raised body temperature)

A rise in body temperature results from a combination of overheating, normally due to exercise, and inadequate fluid intake. A person with hyperthermia will progress through heat exhaustion to heat stroke, with eventual collapse. Heat stroke is an emergency: if the diver is not cooled and rehydrated he or she will die.

Treatment of hyperthermia:
- move the diver as quickly as possible into a cooler place and remove all clothes
- call the emergency services
- sponge the diver's body with a damp cloth and fan him or her manually or with an electric fan
- if the patient is unconscious, put him or her into the recovery position (see page 165) and monitor the ABCs as necessary
- if the patient is conscious you can give him or her a cold drink.

Hypothermia (low body temperature)

Normal internal body temperature is just under 37°C (98.4°F). If for any reason it falls much below this – usually, in diving, because of inadequate protective clothing – progressively more serious symptoms may follow, and the person will eventually die if the condition is not treated rapidly. A drop of 1C° (2F°) causes shivering and discomfort. A 2C° (3F°) drop induces the body's self-heating mechanisms to react: blood flow to the hands and feet is reduced and shivering becomes extreme. A 3C° (5F°) drop results in memory loss, confusion, disorientation, irregular heartbeat and breathing and eventually death.

Treatment of hypothermia:
- move the diver as quickly as possible into a sheltered and warm place; *or:*
- prevent further heat loss: use an exposure bag; surround the diver with buddies' bodies; cover his or her head and neck with a woolly hat, warm towels or anything else suitable
- if you have managed to get the diver into sheltered warmth, remove wet clothing, dress your patient in warm, dry clothing and wrap him or her in an exposure bag or blanket; however, if you are still in the open, the diver is best left in existing garments
- if the diver is conscious and coherent administer a warm shower or bath and a warm, sweet drink
- if the diver is unconscious, check the ABCs (see page 165), call the emergency services, make the patient as warm as possible, and treat for shock (see page 169).

Near-drowning

Near-drowning is a medical condition in which a diver has inhaled some water – water in the lungs interferes with the normal transport of oxygen from the lungs into the bloodstream. A person in a near-drowning condition may be conscious or unconscious.

Near-drowning victims sometimes develop secondary drowning, a condition in which fluid oozing into the lungs causes the diver to drown in internal secretions, so all near-drowning patients must be monitored in a hospital.

Treatment of near-drowning:
- get the diver out of the water and check the ABCs (see page 165); depending on your findings, begin EAR or CPR (see page 166) as appropriate
- if possible, administer oxygen by mask or demand valve
- call the emergency services and get the diver to a hospital for observation, even if he/she appears to have recovered from the experience.

Nitrogen narcosis

Air contains about 80 per cent nitrogen. Breathing the standard diving mixture under compression can lead to symptoms very much like those of drunkenness (nitrogen narcosis is popularly known as 'rapture of the deep'). Some divers experience nitrogen narcosis at depths of 30–40m (100–130ft). Down to a depth of about 60m (200ft) – which is beyond the legal maximum depth for sport-diving in the UK and the USA – the symptoms are not always serious; but below about 80m (260ft) a diver is likely to lose consciousness. Symptoms can occur very suddenly. Nitrogen narcosis is not a serious condition, but a diver suffering from it may do something dangerous.

Treatment of nitrogen narcosis: the only treatment for this condition is to get the diver to ascend immediately to shallower waters.

TRAVELLING MEDICINE

Many doctors decline to issue drugs, particularly antibiotics, to people who want them 'just in case'; but a diving holiday can be ruined by an ear or sinus infection, especially in a remote area or on a live-aboard boat, where the nearest doctor or pharmacy is a long and difficult journey away.

Many travelling divers therefore carry with them medical kits that could lead the uninitiated to think they were hypochondriacs. Nasal sprays, ear drops, antihistamine creams, anti-diarrhoea medicines, antibiotics, sea-sickness remedies . . . Forearmed, such divers can take immediate action as soon as they realize something is wrong. At the very least, this may minimize their loss of diving time.

Always bear in mind that most decongestants and remedies for sea-sickness can make you drowsy and therefore should never be taken before diving.

Shock

Shock is a medical condition and not just the emotional trauma of a frightening experience. Medical shock results from poor blood and oxygen delivery to the tissues. As a result of oxygen and blood deprivation the tissues cannot carry out their functions. There are many causes; the most common is loss of blood.

Treatment for medical shock:
This is directed at restoring blood and oxygen delivery to the tissues:

- check the ABCs (see page 165)
- give 100 per cent oxygen
- control any external bleeding by pressing hard on the wound and/or pressure points (the location of the pressure points is illustrated in first-aid manuals); raise the injured limb or other part of the body
- use a tourniquet only as a last resort and only on the arms and legs
- if the diver is conscious, lay him/her on the back with the legs raised and the head to one side; if unconscious, turn him or her on the left side in the recovery position (see page 165).

MARINE-RELATED AILMENTS

Sunburn, coral cuts, fire-coral stings, swimmers' ear, sea-sickness and bites from various insects are perhaps the most common divers' complaints – but there are more serious marine-related illnesses you should know about.

Cuts and abrasions

Divers should wear appropriate abrasive protection for the undersea environment. Hands, knees, elbows and feet are the areas most commonly affected. The danger with abrasions is that they become infected, so all wounds must be thoroughly washed and rinsed with freshwater and an antiseptic as soon as possible after the injury. Infection may progress to a stage where antibiotics are necessary. If the site of an apparently minor injury becomes inflamed, and the inflammation spreads, consult a doctor immediately – you may need antibiotics to prevent the infection spreading to the bloodstream.

Swimmers' ear

Swimmers' ear is an infection of the external ear canal caused by constantly wet ears. The condition is often a combined fungal and bacterial infection. To prevent it, always dry your ears thoroughly after diving. If you know you are susceptible to the condition, insert drops to dry out the ear after diving. If an infection occurs, the best treatment is to stop diving or swimming for a few days and apply ear drops such as:

- 5 per cent acetic acid in isopropyl alcohol; *or*
- aluminium acetate/acetic acid solution.

FIRST-AID KIT

Your first-aid kit should be waterproof, compartmentalized and sealable, and, as a minimum, should contain the following items:

- a full first-aid manual – the information in this appendix is for general guidance only
- contact numbers for the emergency services
- coins for telephone
- pencil and notebook
- tweezers
- scissors
- 6 large standard sterile dressings
- 1 large Elastoplast/Band-Aid fabric dressing strip
- 2 triangular bandages
- 3 medium-size safety pins
- 1 pack sterile cotton wool
- 2 50mm (2in) crepe bandages
- eyedrops
- antiseptic fluid/cream
- bottle of vinegar
- sachets of rehydration salts
- sea-sickness tablets
- decongestants
- painkillers
- anti-AIDS pack (syringes/needles/drip needle)

Sea or motion sickness

Motion sickness can be an annoying complication on a diving holiday involving boat dives. If you suffer from motion sickness, discuss the problem with a doctor before your holiday – or at least before boarding the boat. But bear in mind that many medicines formulated to prevent travel sickness contain antihistamines, which make you drowsy and will impair your ability to think quickly while you are diving.

Biting insects

Some regions are notorious for biting insects. Take a good insect repellent and some antihistamine cream to relieve the effects.

Sunburn

Be sure to take plenty of precautions against sunburn, which can cause skin cancer. Many people get sunburned on the first day of a holiday and spend a very uncomfortable time afterwards recovering. Pay particular attention to the head, the nose and the backs of the legs. Always use high-protection factor creams, and wear clothes that keep off the sun.

Tropical diseases

Visit the doctor before your trip and make sure you have the appropriate vaccinations for the regions you intend to visit on your trip.

Fish that bite

- **Barracuda** These very rarely bite divers, although they have been known to bite in turbid or murky, shallow water, where sunlight flashing on a knife blade, a camera lens or jewellery has confused the fish into thinking they are attacking their normal prey.

  Treatment: clean the wounds thoroughly and use antiseptic or antibiotic cream. Bad bites will also need antibiotic and anti-tetanus treatment.

- **Moray eels** Probably more divers are bitten by morays than by all other sea creatures added together – usually through putting their hands into holes to collect shells or lobsters, remove anchors, or hide baitfish. Once it bites, a moray often refuses to let go, so you may have to persuade it to by gripping it behind the head and exerting pressure with your finger and thumb until it opens its jaw. You can make the wound worse by tearing your flesh if you pull the fish off.

  Treatment: thorough cleaning and usually stitching. The bites always go septic, so have antibiotics and anti-tetanus available.

- **Sharks** Sharks rarely attack divers, but should always be treated with great respect. Their attacks are usually connected with speared or hooked fish, fish or meat set up as bait, lobsters rattling when picked up, or certain types of vibration, such as that produced by helicopters. The decomposition products of dead fish (even several days old) seem much more attractive to most sharks than fresh blood. Grey reef sharks can be territorial. They often warn of an attack by arching their backs and pointing their pectoral fins downward. Other sharks often give warning by bumping into you first. If you are frightened, a shark will detect this from the vibrations given off by your body. Calmly back up to the reef or boat and get out of the water.

  Treatment: a person who has been bitten by a shark usually has severe injuries and is suffering from shock (see page 169). If possible, stop any bleeding by applying pressure. The patient will need to be stabilized with blood or plasma transfusions before being moved to hospital. Even minor wounds are likely to become infected, so the diver will need antibiotic and anti-tetanus treatment.

- **Triggerfish** Large triggerfish – usually males guarding eggs in 'nests' – are aggressive and will attack divers who get too close. Their teeth can go through rubber fins and draw blood through a 4mm (1/6in) wet suit.

  Treatment: clean the wound and treat it with antiseptic cream.

Venomous sea creatures

Many venomous sea creatures are bottom dwellers – they hide among coral or rest on or burrow into sand. If you need to move along the sea bottom, shuffle along, so that you push such creatures out of the way and minimize the risk of stepping directly onto sharp venomous spines, many of which can pierce rubber fins. Antivenins require specialist medical supervision, do not work for all species, and need refrigerated storage, so they are rarely available when they are needed. Most of the venoms are proteins of high molecular weight that break down under heat.

General treatment: tie a broad bandage at a point between the limb and the body and tighten it. Remember to release it every 15 minutes. Immerse the limb in hot water (perhaps the cooling water from an outboard motor if no other supply is available) at 50°C (120°F) for two hours, until the pain stops. Several injections around the wound of local anaesthetic (such as procaine hydrochloride), if available, will ease the pain. Young or weak people may need CPR (see page 166). Remember that venoms may still be active in fish that have been dead for 48 hours.

- **Cone shells** Live cone shells should never be handled without gloves: the animal has a mobile, tubelike organ that shoots a poison dart. This causes numbness at first, followed by local muscular paralysis, which may extend to respiratory paralysis and heart failure.

  Treatment: tie a bandage between the wound and the body, tighten it, and release it every 15 minutes. CPR (see page 166) may be necessary.

- **Fire coral** Corals of the genus *Millepora* are not true corals but members of the class Hydrozoa – i.e., they are more closely related to the stinging hydroids. Many people react violently from the slightest brush with them – producing blisters sometimes as large as 15cm (6in) across, which can last for as long as several weeks.

  Treatment: bathe the affected part in methylated spirit or vinegar (acetic acid). Local anaesthetic may be required to ease the pain, though antihistamine cream is usually enough.

- **Fireworms** These worms with white hairs along their sides display bristles when touched. These easily break off in the skin, causing a burning feeling and intense irritation.

  Treatment: bathe the affected part in methylated spirit, vinegar (acetic acid) or hot water.

- **Jellyfish** Most jellyfish sting, but few are dangerous. When seasonal changes are favourable you can encounter the Portuguese man-of-war (*Physalia physalis*). These creatures are highly toxic and continued exposure to the stinging cells may require hospital treatment. Sea wasps (*Carybdea alata*) can be found in shallow warm water at night and are attracted to light. These creatures often swarm and stings can be severe, causing muscle cramps, nausea and breathing difficulties. Whenever the conditions are favourable for thimble jellyfish (*Linuche unguiculata*), there is always the chance of much smaller and almost invisible micro-organisms in the water column. Wear protection such as a wet suit or a Lycra skin suit.

Treatment: in the event of a sting, the recommended treatment is to pour acetic acid (vinegar) over both animal and wounds and then to remove the animal with forceps or gloves. CPR (see page 166) may be required.

- **Scorpionfish** These are not considered dangerous in Caribbean waters, but care should always be taken of the spines on top of their dorsal fin.

Treatment: inadvertent stinging can be treated by bathing the affected part of the body in very hot water.

- **Sea urchins** The spines of some sea urchins are poisonous and all sea urchin spines can puncture the skin, even through gloves, and break off, leaving painful wounds that often go septic.

Treatment: for bad cases bathe the affected part of the body in very hot water. This softens the spines, making it easier for the body to reject them. Soothing creams or a magnesium sulphate compress will help reduce the pain, as will the application of the flesh of papaya fruit. Septic wounds need to be treated with antibiotics.

- **Stinging hydroids** Stinging hydroids often go unnoticed on wrecks, old anchor ropes and chains until you put your hand on them, when their nematocysts are fired into your skin. The wounds are not serious but they are very painful, and large blisters can be raised on sensitive skin, which can last for some time.

Treatment: bathe the affected part in methylated spirit or vinegar (acetic acid). Local anaesthetic may

be required to ease the pain, though antihistamine cream is usually enough.

- **Stinging plankton** You cannot see stinging plankton, and so cannot take evasive measures. If there are reports of any in the area, keep as much of your body covered as you can.

Treatment: bathe the affected part in methylated spirit or vinegar (acetic acid). Local anaesthetic may be required to ease the pain, though antihistamine cream is usually enough.

- **Stingrays** Stingrays vary considerably in size from a few centimetres to several metres across. The sting consists of one or more spines on top of the tail; although these point backward they can sting in any direction. The rays thrash out and sting when they are trodden on or caught. The wounds may be large and severely lacerated.

Treatment: clean the wound and remove any spines. Bathe or immerse in very hot water and apply a local anaesthetic if one is available; follow up with antibiotics and anti-tetanus.

Cuts

Underwater cuts and scrapes, especially those caused by coral, barnacles and sharp metal, will usually, if they are not cleaned out and treated quickly, go septic; absorption of the resulting poisons into the body can cause more serious medical conditions.

After every dive, clean and disinfect any wounds, no matter how small. Larger wounds will often refuse to heal unless you stay out of seawater for a couple of days. Surgeonfish have sharp fins on each side of the caudal peduncle; they use these when lashing out at other fish with a sweep of the tail, and they occasionally use them to defend their territory against a trespassing diver. Their 'scalpels' may be covered in toxic mucus, so wounds must be cleaned and treated with antibiotic cream.

As a preventive measure against cuts in general, the golden rule on the reef is: do not touch. Be sure to learn good buoyancy control so that you can avoid touching anything unnecessarily – never forget for an instant that every area of the coral you touch will inevitably be killed.